1977

BEN JONSON

THE
ALCHEMIST

EDITED BY

J. B. STEANE

CAMBRIDGE

AT THE UNIVERSITY PRESS

1967

Published by the Syndics of the Cambridge University Press
Bentley House, 200 Euston Road, London, N.W.1
American Branch: 32 East 57th Street, New York, N.Y. 10022

© Cambridge University Press 1967

Library of Congress Catalogue Card Number: 68–10024

Printed in Great Britain in the City of Oxford
at the Alden Press

CONTENTS

INTRODUCTION

I

The Alchemist is one of the best comedies in English, but many con-
scripted readers may be forgiven if they do not think so. They will
have met the play in a schoolroom and read it 'in class'. They will
have looked ahead to try to make some sense of their own next speech,
lending one ear meanwhile to a Subtle who is only just able to keep
pace with his script, casting one eye at the notes to see if they have
anything to say about a line that might possibly be amusing if it
could be understood, and wishing perhaps that they had listened to
their teacher's synopsis of what was happening 'last period'.

These are always among the trials of play-reading in class, but
with *The Alchemist* they are present to an unusual degree and are also
more than usually regrettable. For *The Alchemist is* an extraordin-
arily good play; good, moreover, in ways that should appeal in
modern times. The pace is brisk, the invention fertile. The comedy
of quick-witted petty criminals who make their living out of fools is
hard-headed and entirely without sentimentality. A series of vividly
drawn characters passes before us, each with his own ambition, each
nosing greedily along a supposed short-cut to fulfilment. One after
another they fall into the traps prepared for them, are gleefully
fleeced by the tricksters, see their little dignities take a tumble, and
still, gluttons for punishment where gain is in view, come back for
more. All this is set against the background of a London where
extremes of wealth and poverty touch, and where a thousand acquisitive wills and wits chafe and strive for the advancement that only
money can ensure.

Six or seven plots are set and kept going; the great supply of words
is always sparkling, never turgid; and embodied in the play is a
moral concern, giving depth and permanent relevance to the social
scene so entertainingly depicted.

Against this we have to note difficulties. First, the very strengths of
the writing, its quick-wit and packed allusiveness, demand that the
reader or listener shall concentrate and make use of his own brain.
The speech has to move, and even in Jonson's own time audiences
are likely to have found themselves fully exercised to keep up with it.
With the passing of three and a half centuries, changes of language
and obscurities of reference that were once readily intelligible are
bound to put an obstacle before the modern reader who attempts an
easy, immediate grasp of detail. It has to be faced, too, that the title
itself, central as it is to the comedy, points to another difficulty.
For the once familiar practices of the alchemist are now as remote
from us as the feudal system or the ptolemaic notion of the universe; and its technicalities are like words in an ancient tongue,

incomprehensible in themselves and often scarcely less baffling when defined.

It is easy to say that we must get beyond this: that we must see the extant force within the extinct form. Certainly the relevance of *The Alchemist* to the modern world should be clear enough. Our own acquisitive society is quite as susceptible to exploitation as were the Londoners of 1610. The prospect of big and easy money makes knaves and fools now as it did then. But Jonson's comedy deals very much in particulars. For example, the precise meaning of 'projection' should be known if we are to realise why Sir Epicure Mammon is in such exalted spirits on this particular day; the two-fold nature of the elixir must be appreciated if we are to see why his imagination soars to the sexual and medical wonders as well as the financial ones that he will perform when he commands its use.

So this is a play for study. One aim of its study should be to make possible the kind of spontaneous enjoyment that Jacobean audiences could find in the play. A good stage performance can give an illusion that this is possible without study, for there is never any feeling that the actors are resuscitating a classic corpse; but full enjoyment still calls on a body of knowledge that a modern audience cannot be expected to possess. Another aim is that with the enjoyment should come first-hand experience of a masterpiece that has its roots more deeply in life than the casual reader will think. And a by-product of all this is that we come to know the London of James and Elizabeth a good deal more intimately than we might after working through volumes of history books.

II

'Alchemy' itself is a word still comfortably within the vocabulary of an educated person, though it probably does not often come out of store. We are likely to know it through such chance acquaintance as is offered by a chemistry textbook:

Alchemy. For some 1,800 years (300 B.C.–A.D. 1500) the transmutation (i.e. conversion) of the base or inexpensive metals into gold and silver was, indeed, the principal object of chemists. Pursued first in Alexandria, and other cities in Egypt, this fantastic quest was taken up with redoubled energy by the Arabs in the eighth and succeeding centuries; and their enthusiasm quickly infected Europe with a passion for *alchemy*[1]

The authors then refer to Chaucer's *Canterbury Tales* where 'numerous fraudulent alchemists who swindled credulous people' are attacked. This is in the Canon's Yeoman's Tale which may be

---

[1] *A Higher School Inorganic Chemistry* (Holmyard and Palmer, 1952).

another source of general knowledge today as it was for Jonson. Or we may meet it in contexts like this from *Julius Caesar*:

> that which would appear offence in us,
> His countenance, like richest alchemy,
> Will change to virtue and to worthiness.
>
> (I, iii, 158–60)

Casca here is talking of Brutus, and saying that it would make all the difference to the conspiracy if they could persuade him to join them: without him the assassination will appear shabby, and conversely his reputation stands so high that people will respect any cause he supports. Brutus's participation will work the miracle that the alchemists tried to achieve through the philosopher's stone. The common metal of their enterprise would change to gold in men's estimation:

> This is the famous stone
> That turneth all to gold

as congregations still sing in George Herbert's hymn.

But 'the famous stone' is not so famous any more. 'We have all heard of alchemists', says Dr Sherwood Taylor, 'and most of us have a picture of them, somewhat confused with that of magicians or wizards.' Certainly 'most of us' would need to have recourse to some book like Dr Taylor's own[1] to gain any understanding of the historical truth, yet Jonson must have been able to assume that his audience would have a knowledge of the technical terms and history of alchemy as well as its principal aims and methods. Without some such knowledge they could hardly appreciate Subtle and Face as the masterly tricksters that they are.

From a period perhaps two hundred years before Christ, the possibilities of changing inferior substances into gold had preoccupied the thoughts of many enterprising and learned men. The philosophical basis of their attempts lay in Aristotle's theories about matter. Every substance, Aristotle held, was essentially constituted of the four elements, air, fire, earth and water. The proportions of these elements were held to differ in every different substance, but all would be present in some degree. It was common observation that one element could be changed by the action of another into a third element different from either: thus the action of fire upon water produces steam which is a kind of air. If the elements themselves can be transformed, it follows that substances made up of these elements may also be changed, and that therefore, for instance, copper, which has some of the properties of gold, might also undergo transmutation—to gold itself, if only the correct processes could be discovered. Ben Jonson's charlatans impose largely on the credulity of simple working-class folk like Dapper and Drugger, but before

[1] *The Alchemists, Founders of Modern Chemistry* (F. Sherwood Taylor, 1951).

(and after) them, generations of scholars, mystics and rulers found the pretensions of the alchemists to be plausible and persuasive. No doubt the desire for money and power spurred them on, but an intellectual assent to what seemed a scientific and even religious endeavour was another encouragement, and this was plentifully forthcoming.

The religious aspect of alchemy had also an ancient and philosophically respectable origin. If matter is transmutable, this must be by divine ordination, and if so great and powerful a blessing as the making of gold is hidden from men's eyes then it must be so by God's will. Therefore only a man specially favoured by God can hope to lay hands on the secret, and such a man must be in a perpetual state of grace. Hence the notion, artfully exploited by Subtle (IV. i.), that the presence of any contaminating worldliness will jeopardise the alchemist's success. In this scene of the play, Subtle has led Sir Epicure Mammon up to the climax of his expectations: one more experiment and the philosopher's stone will be his. But Sir Epicure is discovered in pursuit of Dol Common, and Subtle, acting the part of an outraged holy man, tells him that all may now be lost. An explosion from the laboratory (contrived by Face) confirms the fearful fact, and Subtle exclaims:

> Oh, the cursed fruits of vice and lust!

The rogues here are playing on a tradition centuries old:

> The work which thou expectest to perform
> Will bring thee easily great joy and gain
> When soul and body thou dost beautify
> With chasteness, fasts and purity of mind.
> Avoiding life's distractions and, alone
> In prayerful servitude, giving praise to God.

The lines come from a poem by an alchemist of the eighth century.[1] The association they record between moral purity and alchemical success survived in Jonson's time, and his audiences could savour Subtle's art the better for recognising the tradition that he is skilfully using for his own ends.

True alchemy, then, was reckoned to impose a moral discipline and involve a religious faith, and its character was to a great extent that of a 'mystery': a study that appealed at least as much to the mystic as to the scientist. To Jonson, standing hard-headed and rational at the gate of a freshly enquiring age, the mysticism was nonsense, a dim-witted muddle inherited from the Middle Ages, of use only to rogues and credible only to fools. He does not say this in so many words, for he has no need to. Subtle speaks the jargon, Face plays the awe-struck acolyte, even Dol in her role of learned lady

---

[1] Archelaus: *Upon the Sacred Art*. Translation by C. A. Browne quoted in *Alchemy*, E. J. Holmyard, 1957.

(IV. v.) commands the mystical mumbo-jumbo: all act a parody that is devastatingly close to the original. The alchemist had a priest-like sense of initiation into mysteries. 'The ... wise man speaks in riddles as often as possible', wrote Stephanus of Alexandria, a Greek alchemist of the seventh century. The 'riddles' involved an elaborate system of symbols; so when Surly (II. iii. 182–198) attacks Subtle on the grounds that these terms ('Your toad, your crow, your dragon and your panther') are all so much pretentious nonsense, Subtle replies exactly as the orthodox alchemist would have done: that 'our writers' deliberately 'used to obscure their art', just as the 'choicest fables of the poets' were 'wrapped in perplexed allegory' and the scriptures themselves speak 'oft in parables'. Sir Mammon chips in, ever the eager pupil in these matters:

> Sir, so I told him:
> Because the simple idiot should not learn it
> And make it vulgar.

The comedy here directs us to ridicule not merely the characters concerned, but also the whole body of belief which could prove so convenient to tricksters and so readily acceptable to fools.

The parody *is* very close indeed. 'Your toad, your crow, your dragon and your panther' are among the symbols mocked by Surly, and Jonson has again drawn faithfully on authentic alchemical literature. Here it is George Ripley, the most famous English alchemist of the fifteenth century, whose works are much concerned with the allegorical 'mysteries' of the subject. The changing colours in the various stages of the process of transmutation, for example, are expressed in the very symbols that Surly finds so derisory:

> Pale and black with false citrine,
>   unparfait white and red,
> Peacock's feathers in colours gay, the rainbow
>   which shall overgo
> The spotted panther with the lion green, the crow's
>   bill black as lead;
> These shall appear before the parfit white, and
>   many other moe
> Colours, and after the parfit white, grey and false
>   citrine also:
> And after all this shall appear the blood red
>   invariable,
> Then hast thou a medicine of the third order of his
>   own kind multiplicable.[1]

This is fairly typical, not only of much alchemical writing but also of the relationship between alchemy and *The Alchemist*. Jonson was well-versed in the literature that he laughs at; and his audience, if less learned than the author, would also recognise the comic force of

---

[1] Quoted by Holmyard, op. cit. p. 183.

many details. For us it is necessary at any rate to realise that the details all have point, and that part of the comedy of Subtle's impersonation lies in the very fact that he does it so well. The authenticity of the charlatan in itself ridicules the practice; and, more especially, through the mystical pretensions of alchemy, Jonson ridicules that kind of romantic sensibility which can find a sort of intoxicated satisfaction in the esoteric world of symbols and allegories, dark misty meanings, and a priest-like status for the masters of such mysteries. Sir Epicure Mammon, whose whole soul rises in response to the mystical claims, is just such a romantic; and nobody seems to Jonson a fitter subject for ridicule than he.

The jargon of Ripleyites and Lullianists (cf. II. v. 8–11) may have been old game by 1610, but the particular forms of trickery dramatised in *The Alchemist* were notably topical. Within the memory of many in Jonson's audiences would have been the antics of Edward Kelly and Dr John Dee. Both are mentioned in the play (II. vi. and IV. i.), and their association was not unlike that of Face and Subtle. They practised on an international scale, and Dee, at least, was a genuine scholar. He was a clever man who in his university days produced Aristophanes' comedy *Peace* so ingeniously that 'many vain reports spread abroad of the means [i.e. supernatural means] how that was effected'. Later he became more seriously interested in magic, favourably impressed the Queen, and was said to have warned her against Dr Lopez who was convicted of planning to poison her in 1594. John Aubrey notes about him: 'He used to distill egg-shells, and twas from hence that Ben Jonson had his history of the alchemist, whom he meant.' Dee seems to have been a more worthy person than Subtle, and in his association with Kelly is more gull than guller. Kelly began his career as a crooked lawyer, lasting until about the age of twenty-five when his ears were cut off for the crime of forging or coining. After running into more trouble, he managed to impose on Dr Dee's credulity by invoking a spirit named Uriel who among other things directed the doctor to employ Kelly as his assistant. During the 1580's these two visited various European courts, advertising their occult powers; and Kelly eventually claimed to possess the philosopher's stone, discovered by him at Glastonbury. Like Face and Subtle, Dee and Kelly parted company after a quarrel. Kelly died in prison (see notes on IV. i. 90) and Dee lived on till 1608, two years before Jonson's play. The theory that these two were the prototypes of Subtle and Face receives some support from the presence of a third impostor, Albert Laski, who joined the other two in their European séances, making up an 'indenture tripartite' to compare with Dol's contribution in the play. Speculation on the matter is not very profitable; but it is interesting to note that the kind of trickery Jonson dramatises found its exponents and victims in real life, and that his audience would see a recognisable reality in the farcical events of the play.

Some of the other events were even more recent than this. Nothing may seem more unlikely to a modern audience than that Dapper should receive so credulously the news that his aunt is 'Queen of the Fairies'; but two cases are recorded of very similar swindles occurring at just about this time. One of them[1] concerns another trio of tricksters, Sir Anthony and Saul Ashley, and a man called Greene, who promised a Dorset farmer, Thomas Rogers, that he should meet the Queen of the Fairies and marry her. Greene was to arrange this and Rogers gave him money to that end. The case came to Chancery in November 1609 and was finished in February 1610. Then in 1613 there came up at the Old Bailey a case in which John and Alice West, 'falsely called the King and Queen of Fairies', were convicted of various 'notorious and lewd cosenages', among them the gulling of a certain Thomas Moore and his wife. Some of the details are quoted by Herford and Simpson in the notes to their edition of the play:[2]

> They brought him into a vault, where they showed him two attired like the King and Queen of Fairies, and by them little elves and goblins, and in the same place an infinite company of bags, and upon them written 'This is for Thomas Moore', 'This is for his wife', but would not let him touch anything.

Fact here seems elaborately stranger than fiction. But there it is: such things were done on Albion's shore, and Jonson's comedy of fraud is not quite the fantastical gallimaufry it might seem.

III

Alchemy, however, is essentially a vehicle in the play: the centre of interest lies elsewhere, and Jonson is using the particular subject of alchemy as the means to another end. Other kinds of trickery might have sufficed, certainly other ways in which men could be exhibited as capable of infinite self-degradation when confronted with the prospect of easy money. For this is what we see in *The Alchemist* as in *Volpone*, the other great comedy, and it is fundamental to Jonson's work as social critic. He took himself very seriously in this role:

> I'll strip the ragged follies of the time
> Naked as at their birth.

So says Asper in *Every Man Out of his Humour*, a character described as 'an ingenious and free spirit, eager and constant in reproof, without fear controlling the world's abuses'. This is very much how Jonson saw himself, and in a long series of plays he tore fairly ruthlessly at 'the follies of the time', holding up, as he thought, the mirror to truth, and letting folk see their corruption in all its nakedness.

[1] Quoted, by Professor C. J. Sisson: 'A Topical Reference in "The Alchemist"'. *J. Q. Adams Memorial Studies* (1948).
[2] *The Works of Ben Jonson*, ed. C. H. Herford and P. Simpson (London, 1925–52), Vol. X, p. 98. The text of *The Alchemist* is found in Vol. V.

He does it perhaps most effectively in *Volpone*. Here we see a magnifico of Venice pretend that he is mortally sick. Around him come men and women who hope to inherit his wealth. Greedy as they are, they nevertheless present him with gold and precious stones, for they think these will prove a good investment. More than this, we see that a father will disinherit his son and a jealous husband will prostitute his wife rather than lose the glittering prize which he believes is so nearly his. Still more savage is the exposure of Voltore, the lawyer. He is a grave public man, ponderous and pompous in his eloquence; also careful of his dignity, for in its preservation lies his fee (and 'his soul moves in his fee'). Yet, because the wealth he covets seems to demand it, he is willing to humiliate himself in the court, fall down in a pretended fit, seeming to be 'possessed' by an epilepsy. And he is indeed 'possessed'; not by the fit he is simulating but by the wealth he so desires. Later, another character picks up the word, in lines which might be the motto of the play:

> These possess wealth, as sick men possess fevers,
> Which trulier may be said to possess them.

The Alchemist too dramatises this kind of 'possession'. Because they see Lovewit's house as a gold mine, the gulls who come visiting are obsessed with the single idea of gain, and this is now their 'humour'. The famous Jonsonian explanation of 'humours' occurs in this passage:

> As when some one peculiar quality
> Doth so possess a man, that it doth draw
> All his affects, his spirits and his powers
> In their confluctions, all to run one way,
> This may be truly said to be a humour.
> (*Every Man Out of his Humour*)

Dapper, Mammon, Drugger, Kastril and Tribulation Wholesome are by nature very different characters, but in their besotted condition they essentially share a common 'humour': all the confluctions run one way, possessed by the greed for wealth. The dapper little clerk forgets his carefully studied city nonchalance ('I had a scurvy writ or two to make, And I had lent my watch last night to one that dines today at the sheriff's') and becomes a goggling simpleton, to be bound, gagged, pinched and robbed, thrust into the jakes and there forgotten. The fastidious aristocrat forgets the restraints and good sense that according to his friend Surly are part of his normal self:

> Heart! Can it be
> That a grave sir, a rich, that has no need,
> A wise sir, too, at other times, should thus
> With his own oaths and arguments make hard means
> To gull himself?

Similarly the small shopkeeper will forget normal business prudence, the countryman will 'thump' his sister into making a ridiculous marriage, and the religious zealot will twist logic and principle, the Bible and his own soul, all so as not to be cheated of the wealth that is in reality cheating them. *The Alchemist*, like *Volpone*, is a play about possession.

It also, through these individuals, depicts a society: a civilisation at a particular stage of development.[1] As Subtle casts his spell chanting the word 'projection', so the capitalists, 'the projectors' of the new economic order, had begun to assume the powers of the social magician. The rise of capitalism put before men's eyes exciting prospects of private enrichment by private enterprise. The jostle and thrust of competition that is inevitable in any centre of power became particularly fierce in the London of the early seventeenth century. For centuries the basis of power had been possession of land and rank; now it was money. Not that this was entirely new. The Malta of Marlowe's play about the famous Jew is essentially the London of his own time and of Jonson's twenty years later:

> *Governor*: Welcome, great Bashaws, how fares Calymath?
> What wind drives you thus into Malta-road?
> *Bashaw*: The wind that bloweth all the world besides,
> Desire of gold.
>
> (1420–23)

But by the early 1600's, London had become much more extravagantly and strenuously a place where individuals made money to cut a dash in order to obtain influence and so make more money. Jonson was the great chronicler of this. In *The Devil is an Ass* (1616) a devil who visits London exclaims: 'hell is a grammar school to this'. In *Volpone* the theme is stated more fully:

> Riches, the dumb god, that giv'st all men tongues,
> Thou canst do nought, and yet mak'st men do all things.

In *The Alchemist* we see the capitalist ideal in a more comic light, with the figure of Sir Epicure Mammon prancing excitedly in it:

> Come on, sir. Now you set your foot on shore
> In *Novo Orbe*. Here's the rich Peru:
> And there within, sir, are the golden mines,
> Great Solomon's Ophir! He was sailing to't
> Three years, but we have reached it in ten months.
> This is the day, wherein to all my friends
> I will pronounce the happy word: Be rich!'.
> This day you shall be *Spectatissimi*.

But if Sir Epicure is a donkey, so is society, for it too is led on by the carrot called money. It too lends itself to exploitation by clever cheats; and it too is after a reward that is a cheat in itself.

[1] On this see L. C. Knights, *Drama and Society in the Age of Jonson* (London, 1937, Peregrine Books, 1962).

Now this much, a comedy directed against false values, folly and trickery, covers, I think, only a part of the attitude to life which *The Alchemist* expresses. This much is readily acceptable as sound morality, and when it is enforced by all the arts of the poetic dramatist, as here, the effect is great. But the play's 'morality' is more complicated than this, less orthodox and more interesting.

In an essay in *Scrutiny* (IX. 3) called *Crime and Punishment in Ben Jonson*, D. J. Enright wrote of *The Alchemist* that it 'has not the fine unity' of *Volpone*. He continues:

> The end, when Lovewit comes along and quite irresponsibly snaps up Dame Pliant from under Surly's nose (Surly is a very half-hearted character altogether) and even more irresponsibly turns a blind eye to Face's misbehaviour, is not far above the level of *Bartholomew Fair* [described earlier as 'a frivolous play']. It will not bear comparison with the end of *Volpone*.

'Crime and punishment' is a useful heading, and it is certainly interesting to see how the theme is treated in the three comedies just mentioned. In *Volpone* the criminals are punished severely: Mosca goes to the galleys, Volpone to prison, and various humiliating penalties are inflicted upon the gulls themselves. In a last speech the lesson is sent home:

> Now you begin,
> When crimes are done and past, and to be punished,
> To think what your crimes are: away with them.
> Let all that see these vices thus rewarded
> Take heart and love to study 'em! Mischiefs feed
> Like beasts, till they be fat, and then they bleed.

The judgment is authoritative, and the last image neatly summarises the plot, reminding us, incidentally, of the 'Argument' poem preceding *The Alchemist*. The mischief-makers here go about their business till with trick piled on trick there comes an explosion, 'and they, and all, in fume are gone'. But when they (Subtle, Face and Dol) 'are gone', it is not with the harsh judgment of these lines in *Volpone* ringing in our ears. On the contrary, their offences are palliated: Subtle and Dol lose their loot but escape the law, and Face not only retains his position but has his master Lovewit connive at the trickery for which orthodox morality would say he deserved punishment.

In his explicit statements, Jonson was a sternly sincere, orthodox moralist. In such plays as *Volpone, Sejanus* and *Catiline* evil is fully exhibited, given its scope and judged. *The Alchemist*, which seems to Mr Enright less satisfying partly for the reason that the crime is virtually left unpunished, seems to me rather more interesting, and ultimately stronger, partly for the very reason that the morality is less bluntly unambiguous, and in fact less orthodox.

Of course Subtle, Face and Dol are tricksters, and of course we

see them as anti-social, irresponsible, unprincipled even among themselves, and so forth. There is no sentimental creation of the 'lovable
rogue' or the 'whore with a heart of gold'. These people yelp and
snarl at each other in the opening scene, and remain predatory
creatures, less than civilised, less than fully human, throughout. On
the other hand, they are infinitely resourceful and entertaining; the
energy, thought, wit and action seem inexhaustible. Moreover, in all
their confrontations with the rest of the world we are placed on *their*
side rather than on the other: the fun of their schemes and the folly
of their victims make us turn a much more tolerant eye on their
doings than orthodox morality soberly permits. And in this we are
being worked upon in the spirit of the master, Lovewit, who, when
he sees these enormities, is more amused than outraged.

Lovewit does not appear in the play until the last act, but his
position is crucial. D. J. Enright, in the passage quoted, says that
Lovewit behaves irresponsibly, and so by the standards of *Volpone*
he does. But Lovewit is what his name proclaims him to be. 'I love a
teeming wit as I love my nourishment', he says, and consequently he
places a high value upon his butler Face, and surveys the whole
social scene with a relish that has little or nothing of the moralist about
it. Lovewit's arrival in the play is like that of the *deus ex machina*. We
have heard of him long ago in Act I:

> Oh, fear not him. While there dies one a week
> O' the plague, he's safe from thinking toward London.
> Beside, he's busy at his hop-yards now;
> I had a letter from him. If he do,
> He'll send such word for airing o' the house
> As you shall have sufficient time to quit it.

Very faintly, the religious overtone makes itself felt: 'watch ye therefore: for ye know not when the master of the house cometh . . .'.
Meanwhile like naughty children in the absence of their parents, the
trio of rogues use the house left in Face's care; they dress up, have
people in, play game after game till they nearly come to blows, and
then scurry about frantically to put the place straight before the
master can find out about them. Inevitably there is some suggestion
of a parable about such a plot. But however subdued the suggestion,
and however comic the context, it still places Lovewit in this very
important position: that of the master whose power is formidable and
whose judgment may come like the wrath of God unexpectedly from
on high. So by his status in the plot, Lovewit's judgment should be
the one which we as audience are called on to respect.

Mr Enright found Lovewit's judgment unsatisfactory and the
ending flawed therefore. Another writer, Edward Partridge in *The
Broken Compass*,[1] argues that Lovewit is intentionally presented in a
bad light and that the author is judging him too. I do not believe it;

[1] Chatto and Windus, 1958.

for it is not only Lovewit's position in the plot that confers this authority upon him. It is also the prevailing spirit of fun which makes *The Alchemist* something different from the moral play that both these critics want it to be.

Supporting this is the odd treatment of the sceptic, Surly. Surly is Lovewit's opposite number. He condemns what Lovewit condones and scowls where Lovewit smiles. Yet their dramatic function is alike in this, that both are judges. Surly is intelligent and strong enough to be proof against Subtle; he is even able for a while to gull the gullers. But the working of the drama accords him very little respect. When he appears in his Spanish disguise we laugh at him more than with him, even though we know that he is for the time outwitting Face and Subtle. He cuts a ridiculous figure and they are amusing at his expense. Then finally his plans come to nothing and in the end he stands glumly, a butt for Lovewit's gibes, having lost the game because he was not quick-witted enough to keep pace. There is right-mindedness in his scowls, an admirably rational scepticism in his determination not to be gulled; but the final impression is that he too, like Lovewit, is defined by his name. And whereas Lovewit has life in his name and nature, Surly is heavy and has no touch of that zest and relish which in the judgment of Lovewit (and, I think, the play) go far to redeem the rogues.

The rogues themselves ought, in an orthodox morality, to be merely ruthless and despicable. Instead, we find ourselves laughing with them too often. Moreover, if we laugh it is in appreciation of a kind of mind. For example, Face in the first scene attacks Subtle, reminding him of what he was when he (Face) met him:

> at Pie-corner,
> Taking your meal of steam in from cooks' stalls,
> Where, like the father of hunger, you did walk,
> Piteously costive, with your pinch'd-horn nose
> And your complexion of the Roman wash,
> Stuck full of black and melancholic worms,
> Like powder-corns shot at the Artillery Yard . . .
> When you went pinned up in the several rags
> You had raked and picked from dunghills before day,
> Your feet in mouldy slippers for your kibes,
> A felt of rug and a thin threaden cloak
> That scarce would cover your no-buttocks . . .

The mind that can depict with this kind of vividness is at any rate wonderfully alive. He draws a caricature of Subtle ('your complexion . . . like powder-corns shot at the Artillery Yard') with a Dickensian attack and sureness. The language takes its substance from the world around: a mind evidently open-eyed and keenly receptive to the sights of the city. Each of the little pictures has its own vigour: the picture, for instance, of the wretched man searching through the 'dunghills before day' is given pictorial life by the verb 'raked', strong and specific. One idea generates another; so that we see 'your feet in mouldy slippers', which is external and part of the general caricature, and then look underneath them to the chilblains ('for your kibes') chafing miserably in their rawness.

This vitality of speech is inseparable from the character of the speaker: Face is not just a 'bad character' who happens to be given lively lines. We, as audience, warm to the liveliness, and therefore to the character; and so it is throughout the play, for Face's vitality never flags. The same is true of Subtle and Dol. After Face's denunciation just quoted, Subtle replies, painting a brilliant picture of the butler-on-the-make. The wit is quick and fertile, the images are specific and the lines packed. Characters whose speech can dazzle in this way, keeping an audience on its mettle, must command a kind of respect. We see them also as artists. Subtle, Pygmalionlike, has created Face, he claims:

> Have I ta'en thee out of dung . . .
> Raised thee from brooms and dust and watering-pots?
> Sublimed thee and exalted thee and fixed thee
> I' the third region called our state of grace?
> Wrought thee to spirit, to quintessence, with pains
> Would twice have won me the philosopher's work.
> Put thee in words and fashion? Made thee fit
> For more than ordinary fellowships?

Professor Partridge, in *The Broken Compass*, notes that these are alchemic terms, and comments: 'Subtle claims to have alchemised a man.' He sees this as 'impiety', with Subtle as 'a parody of the Creator' and the jargon as 'a parody of the Word'. Possibly so; but I cannot believe that the 'impiety' was ever taken very seriously by any audience—there is too much amusement. And as the scene proceeds there is every inducement for the audience to identify themselves with the rogues. It is Dol who has the last word in the argument. She harangues formidably, a low-life Queen Bess, and proposes a programme full of promise for their entertainment and ours:

> Shall we go make
> A sort of sober, scurvy, precise neighbours,
> That scarce have smiled twice sin' the King came in,
> A feast of laughter at our follies?

The 'feast of laughter' is to be our own too, and of course we relish the prospect and warm to these quick-witted providers of the feast. Professor Partridge speaks of their 'impiety' and 'pretentiousness of language', seeing them as 'animals which live on a lower plane than men', and he remarks that Face 'is really [only] the clothes he has on'. But there are far more powerful forces working to counteract this heavily moralistic reaction: and chief among these is laughter. We laugh *with* the trickers: they are the entertainers, and every speech

B

that is put into their mouths expresses energy, humour and life. They
pipe, and the foolish human race jigs to their tune. Mammon,
Kastril, Ananias, Drugger are all entertaining characters, but they
are put in motion, made to dance in their ludicrous way for us, by the
ingenuities of the three. They are the hosts at this 'feast of laughter'
and by the fifth act they have so conditioned us to the appreciation
of 'a teeming wit' that we are quite prepared, dramatically, to accept
Lovewit's 'irresponsible' judgment when he makes it.

IV

This does not mean that Jonson is an irresponsible moralist here, or
that *The Alchemist* is 'mere' entertainment. It is a very highly organ-
ised, sharply pointed moral comedy, but its sting is directed not so
much at the exploiters as at the society which by its greed and folly
is so open to exploitation. And, of course, the rogues themselves are
quite firmly 'placed'. However great their vitality, we are left in no
doubt about the limitations of their humanity. There is no depth and
no loyalty about them. Their horizon is narrow and their values are
often flashy and vulgar. In the speech quoted on page 13, Subtle
claims to have created Face ('ta'en thee out of dung') and made him
'fit for more than ordinary fellowships':

> Given thee thy oaths, thy quarrelling dimensions,
> Thy rules to cheat at horse-race, cock-pit, cards,
> Dice, or whatever gallant tincture else.

This, to them, is the crown of creation; this is what life is for—
cutting a dash among the sporting lads and cheating better than they
can. Jonson is perfectly realistic and truthful about these people:
their native wit and vitality are remarkable, but social and economic
conditions (and we are made strongly aware of them) have con-
stricted and contorted them so that their lives are confined within the
narrow limits of petty crime.

It would be all too easy, however, for the professedly respectable,
virtuous folk in Jonson's audiences to spend their condemnation on
this small game, and to miss the broader and more unsettling social
criticism that the play presents.

The gulls are so varied as to show in cross-section a society led
by greed and lust to folly and loss. The nobleman, the countryman,
the little clerk, the churchman, the small shopkeeper: Jonson's net
is cast widely enough over society to take in all these. Morally the
scope is equally wide. Their faults include: greed and lust, excess,
triviality; coarseness, thickheadedness; false ambition, credulity and
feeble submissiveness; hypocrisy, double-think and extortion; mere
silliness. The frailties of the race are on show. But what might have
been a parade of assorted vices gains unity and purpose from the
motive that is common to all of them: an obsessive desire for easy

money. In this way the play does more than offer a rich collection of satirical portraits; it depicts a whole society, ruthlessly individualistic and acquisitive, and ultimately deluded and impoverished by its own false values.

Eminent among the gulls is Sir Epicure Mammon. He is one of Jonson's best creations, a fantastic who is as real as the fantasy world that he inhabits will let him be. His language is fervent and lyrical—and ridiculous. Its swelling, intoxicated extravagance has something of 'that fine madness ... Which rightly should possess a poet's brain', as Drayton wrote of Marlowe. The verse too has the kind of glamour associated with Marlowe's Tamburlaine. But when Tamburlaine's words are put into the mouth of an effete, self-indulgent and foolish knight they lose somewhat in dignity, and it is Jonson's intention that they should. He wrote Sir Epicure's lines with an unrestrained lyricism that is rare for him; but they are there for laughter and, ultimately, for condemnation. It is partly that the character of the speaker is ludicrously unworthy of 'the mighty line'; partly that the Marlovian style is itself perilously close to the ridiculous, a fact that would be apparent to the more sophisticated audience twenty years after Marlowe's own time; partly too that Surly is on the stage, commenting in the style of the sceptical modern and so making Sir Epicure appear still more the old-fashioned woolly-headed romantic. Above all there is the precise force of the words themselves:

> I will have all my beds blown up, not stuffed;
> Down is too hard. And then, mine oval room
> Filled with such pictures as Tiberius took
> From Elephantis, and dull Aretine
> But coldly imitated. Then my glasses,
> Cut in more subtle angles, to disperse
> And multiply the figures as I walk
> Naked between my succubae. My mists
> I'll have of perfume, vapoured 'bout the room
> To lose ourselves in; and my baths like pits
> To fall into, from whence we will come forth
> And roll us dry in gossamer and roses.
> (Is it arrived at ruby?)—Where I spy
> A wealthy citizen or rich lawyer
> Have a sublimed pure wife, unto that fellow
> I'll send a thousand pound, to be my cuckold.

Greed for wealth is so much the unifying factor in *The Alchemist* that it almost seems an end in itself, but Sir Epicure reminds us that the play's attack extends to the delusive ways of life that folk propose to themselves as ends. Here mammon is the means; the complete epicure the end. The bed and the table become the twin centres of life, and Sir Epicure has plenty to say about the gourmet's diet later. The bed promotes the two Deadly Sins of Sloth and Lechery. 'Down is too hard' for the realisation of Sir Epicure's ideal and yet by normal

values it is a synonym for softness (as in Jonson's own lyric: 'Have
you felt the wool of beaver, Or swansdown ever'). The corollary of
aspiration is discontent, and the man who today calls swansdown
hard will tomorrow be complaining that air is adamantine. However,
'beds blown up' are at one with the euphorically inflated imagination
which now wanders off along the twisted blind-alleyways of sensuality.
Connoisseurs of pornographic art generally regarded Aretine as the
last word. To Sir Epicure, already far advanced in the connoisseur's
superior boredom, Aretine is 'dull'. The looking-glasses that will
stimulate his sensuality and satisfy his vanity suggest the most sterile
of perversions; a self-regarding indulgence remote even from sensual
passion. The 'succubae' are unequivocally sinister. And even though
we now return to the 'pleasant', high-poetic images of perfumed
mists, baths, gossamer and rubies, we are still aware of the spiritual
price of these luxuries. The mists are 'to lose ourselves in' (as the
succubae take the man's soul from him); and the pits (in religious
symbolism traps of Satan's devising) are to 'roll' in (cf. Milton's 'roll
with pleasure in a sensual sty', *Comus*, 77). So the high-living which
seems designed to make man more than man will only make him
less; and just in case we are finding this eloquence too infectious,
Jonson now pricks the bubble with Mammon's comically down-to-
earth, greedy self-interruption, asking what is going on in the
laboratory—'Is it arrived at ruby?'. Then, so that we should not have
any easy-going inclination to say 'Well, it's his business, let him get
on with it', we are sharply reminded that the money spent gratifying
corrupt tastes will soon be spent on the corruption of others: if any
citizen have a Lucretia for a wife, she shall be bought, for 'the dumb
god, riches . . . [makes] men do all things'.

Sir Epicure's colourful fantasies and poetic raptures should not,
then, deceive us into thinking that he has 'run away with' his
creator. The author's judgment is firm, and in the division that was
to grow wider through the next decades the standards of this judgment are closer to the puritan mind than to the cavalier. In other
ways, Jonson was very anti-Puritan, not only in his own life, but in
his works, and in this play particularly.

When Dol proposes the 'feast of laughter' as the day's and the
play's programme, she specifies that it is to be at the expense of

> A sort of sober, scurvy, precise neighbours,
> That scarce have smiled twice sin' the King came in.

'Precise' meant puritanical, and the 'precisian' was a character often
satirised by pamphleteers and playwrights of this period (they
wanted to close the theatres, for one thing). Of Jonson's 'precisions',
Ananias is a figure of fun, but Wholesome is something worse. He is
an Elder of his Church, and this little extra power and intelligence
have made him worldly wise in the ways of compromise. He wants
'the stone', for it will bring more power: the kingdom of the Saints

will come about, and this will naturally inaugurate the millenium for
righteous folk in general but for the Elders in particular. So admirable
must this end seem, that almost any means can be justified to attain
it; so the ambitious Pastor will persuade himself and, if need be,
others. Ananias, simple soul that he is, has picked up a moral
slogan:

> The sanctified cause
> Should have a sanctified course.

But the more sophisticated Wholesome is well able to put him right
on that one. He rationalises skilfully:

> Not always necessary.
> The children of perdition are oft-times
> Made instruments even of the greatest works

and Jonson, in an ecstasy of irony, makes Ananias exclaim:

> I have not edified more, truly, by man,
> Not since the beautiful light first shone on me.

Dapper, Drugger and Kastril provoke milder satire, though each
makes a contribution to the humour. Dapper is characterised in his
first scene with several deft touches. He arrives with something that
in his mouth has very much the air of a prepared speech. He has
acquired a little swagger and a few modish terms, and affects the
offhand bored manner of the man-about-town:

> I had a scurvy writ or two to make,
> And I had lent my watch last night to one
> That dines today at the sheriff's, and so was robbed
> Of my pass-time.

But then we see the pose droop as with naive awe he goggles at 'the
alchemist' who has entered in cap and gown:

> Is this the cunning man?

Face proceeds to reduce him further with a patronising, quietly
satirical thumb-nail sketch in this speech of introduction to Subtle:

> a special gentle,
> That is the heir to forty marks a year,
> Consorts with the small poets of the time,
> Is the sole hope of his old grandmother.

His petty ambitions are exploited mercilessly by the two tricksters,
and finally the dapper little front of the man is stripped as he is
thrust, bound and gagged but still hopeful, into 'Fortune's privy
lodgings'.

Drugger, the tobacconist, may seem the least vivid of the characters, yet this is the part that famous actors from Garrick onwards
have chosen for themselves. One suspects that they may be attracted
to it for bad reasons. If there is less character in Drugger's lines than

in those of, say, Mammon, Kastril or Ananias, there is also more scope for the actor to create his own 'imposed' characterisation. There comes then a rare opportunity for scene-stealing; and Garrick's famous portrayal evidently indulged in more 'business' than most modern producers would be keen to allow him. A vivid account by a contemporary critic is included in the Memoir which precedes *The Private Correspondence of David Garrick* and is quoted by Herford and Simpson:[1]

> Abel Drugger's first appearance would disconcert the muscular economy of the wisest. His attitude, his dread of offending the doctor, his saying nothing, his gradual stealing in farther and farther, his impatience to be introduced, his joy to his friend Face, are imitable by none. Mr Garrick has taken that walk to himself, and is the ridiculous above all conception. When he first opens his mouth, the features of his face seem, as it were, to drop upon the tongue; it is all caution; it is timorous, stammering and inexpressible. When he stands under the conjuror to have his features examined, his teeth, his beard, his little finger, his awkward simplicity, and his concern, mixed with hope and fear, joy and avarice, and good-nature, are above painting.

Garrick toned down the absurdities of his predecessor in the part, Theophile Cibber, but retained a piece of 'business', originated accidentally by Cibber, in which Drugger in his nervousness breaks the urinal bottle in Subtle's room. In all of this (quite apart from the additions he wrote for Drugger's part and the cuts he made in other roles) Garrick was imposing on the play. Modern practice continues, I think, to impose an interpretation foreign to Jonson. Drugger is not vicious, certainly, but he is a dim-wit and is still a subject for satire. His foolishness asks for gulling just as the others do, and to make a winsome show-stealing star-turn out of him is a betrayal of the play's unsentimentality.

There remain Kastril and his 'suster', Dame Pliant. Pliant is a feeble-minded creature, at one moment heavy with prejudice:

> Truly, I shall never brook a Spaniard . . .
> Never sin' eighty-eight could I abide 'em,
> And that was some three year afore I was born, in truth.

yet intimidated into acquiescence about twenty lines later. Kastril, 'the angry boy', is a marvellous portrayal of the country gull, a familiar type in comedies and pamphlets of this time, but here done with rare relish and a fine sense of fun in such matters as his delicate encouragement of Dame Pliant:

> Ass, my suster,
> Go kuss him as the cunning man would ha' you.
> I'll thrust a pin i' your buttocks else.

This element of fun does not cancel the greedy brutishness of the man. He too is one on whose silly, boorish nature the sillier and cruder side of city life is having its effect. He too is part of the satire. We do, however, look at these vivid minor characters with less seriousness. Jonson is out, in this and his next comedy, to catch all the fun of the fair; and the Kastrils, Druggers and Dappers are part of it. As is more true of *Bartholomew Fair* and far less true of *Volpone*, Jonson conveys a sense that we must not scowl too humourlessly at these things. In *Bartholomew Fair* there is one character who stalks through the fair frowning and noting the various 'enormities' he sees about him. He is Justice Overdo; his name describes him and he is himself a subject for satire. *The Alchemist* is a moralist-comedy with teeth in it. It bites deep into many vices and follies, and engages in a thoughtful audience a much more serious interest than 'mere entertainment' will provide. But it is an entertainment none the less, and if, as critics, we look only at the exposure of the enormities and miss the fun of the feast, we are missing a good deal in Ben Jonson.

V

The play brought out much of the best in its author. In many of his long contentious days he seems to have been a cantankerous, self-opinionated man; and in some of his writings the blustering, brow-beating manner is tiresomely insistent. *The Alchemist* is not one of these. He was also a person capable of rare good sense and good humour. As an observer of his times he was without equal among writers, and, once he felt himself established and without the need to be defensive or aggressive, his sensibility matured so that the involvement of his moral judgment was that of a thinker deeply concerned with the condition of society and the individual man. *The Alchemist*, with *Volpone* and perhaps *Sejanus*, is among the best works of this maturity.

He was also a very distinguished scholar. Step-son of a master bricklayer, he was lucky enough to go to Westminster School and benefit from the teaching and later the friendship of William Camden; but he never went to either university, though he tells us he received honorary degrees from both. All his life he kept up his studies, and in middle age boasted with probable justice that he was 'better versed and knew more in Greek and Latin than all the poets in England and quintessenceth their brains'. One monument to his learning is the reference system in his classical tragedies, *Sejanus* and *Catiline*; every literary source is noted and the scholarship is broad and scrupulous. It is this kind of thing (the feature in which he probably took most pride) that gave him in later centuries the reputation of being a dully academic writer. In his essay of 1919, T. S. Eliot said:

> The reputation of Jonson has been of the most deadly kind that can be compelled upon the memory of a great poet. To be universally accepted; to be damned by the praise that quenches all

desire to read the book; to be afflicted by the imputation of the
virtues which excite the least pleasure; and to be read only by
historians and antiquaries—this is the most perfect conspiracy of
approval.[1]

No play can have done more to correct this than *The Alchemist*, yet
even here the scholarly mind is apparent. The alchemical terms are
all correctly used, and the many allusions accurately reflect their
curious sources. It is not surprising that the play was a great success
at Oxford in 1610, when even the theologians flocked to the theatre,
presumably quite ready to savour the scholar-playwright's wit at the
expense of the anabaptists.

The treatment of Ananias and Wholesome has exactly that kind of
easy sureness that some of the earlier satirical portraits lack. One feels
that *The Alchemist* was written in confidence, while plays like *Every
Man Out of His Humour* (1599 or early 1600), *Cynthia's Revels* and
The Poetaster (both 1601) are bulging with material that his personal
interests failed to completely discipline. These were the years of the
dramatists' wars. Jonson's particular enemies then were Thomas
Dekker and John Marston, but he seems at this time to have had a
fairly low opinion of the world in general. In 1603 a young lawyer
called John Massingham wrote in his diary: 'Ben Jonson the poet
now lives upon one Townshend [Sir Robert Townshend] and scorns
the world.'

There is too much protesting in these early plays, too much self-
awareness. Out of the skirmishing and sniping the modern reader is
not likely to gain much pleasure. The plots are bad, the language is
difficult and not very rewarding, the characters are irritating more
often than entertaining. Occasionally there is a good polemical
passage, occasionally a fine lyric, but that, for most tastes, must be
about all. One good thing that emerged from the war, however, was
the maliciously vivid description of Jonson's appearance by Dekker
in his *Satiromastix*. His face 'looks for all the world like a rotten
apple when tis bruised'; he talks 'i' the nose'; and 'it's cakes and
pudding to me to see his face make faces when he reads his Songs and
Sonnets'. Later we return to this rotten russet apple of a face: this
time it is 'full of pocky-holes and pimples' and, for good measure,
'punched full of oylet-holes, like the cover of a warming pan'.

With a face like that, one would have to fight or go under. Jonson
was a great fighter, and not only in words, for he went with the army
to Flanders in 1596, taking as he said 'opima spolia' and winning a
duel fought 'in the face of both the camps'. He also fought the actor
Gabriel Spencer and killed him in Hoxton Fields beyond Shoreditch,
escaping the gallows only on the plea of benefit of clergy and being
branded on the thumb instead. But all his life he was the kind of
man who inspired great devotion in some and enmity in others. The

---

[1] T. S. Eliot, *Selected Essays*, London, 1932, p. 147.

'dramatists' war' of the early nineties has been mentioned. In later years the arch-enemy was Inigo Jones, the most famous artist and architect of his day. Jones and Jonson had collaborated for the first time in the Christmas of 1604 for *The Masque of Blackness*. The association was a brilliant one and it continued on and off till 1630, the year of *Love's Triumph through Callipolis*. Of all entertainments, Masques depend most on a fine balance being preserved among the contributing arts, and Jonson's policy was emphatically to establish the poet as most senior partner. Jones' success and the resources that were placed at his disposal became a great aggravation to Jonson's temper and the two quarrelled bitterly, expostulations, epigrams and parodies flowing from Jonson's pen. He told Drummond of Hawthornden that 'he said to Prince Charles of Inigo Jones, that when he wanted words to express the greatest villain in ye world he would call him ane Inigo'. And Jonson's catalogue of villains was not short of names.

All this quarrelling no doubt generated energy as well as consuming it. Jonson's energy anyway seems to have been practically inexhaustible. In 1618 it took him on foot to Scotland, mountain belly, forty-five years and all. There he received many honours, including a dinner which cost the City of Edinburgh £221 6s. 4d., and went on to Hawthornden, the estate of William Drummond, poet, scholar and gentleman. Jonson drained his cellars (drink, said Drummond, was 'one of the elements in which he liveth') and talked. Drummond made notes of these conversations if they can be called that, for he himself seems to have played little part. They tell much about Jonson's life and opinions: 'Shakespeare lacked art', 'John Donne the first poet in the world in some things . . . for not being understood would perish', and he (Jonson) 'wrote all his verses first in prose for so his master Camden had learned him'. Interesting too is Drummond's summary of Jonson's character: 'he is passionately kind and angry, careless either to gain or keep; vindictive, but if well answered, at himself'. Above all one has the impression of a vast assertive vitality, the energy that, after all, was to keep him going, writing, quarrelling, drinking, holding court as literary dictator of the Devil Tavern, and still living on until his almost penniless last days in 1637. He had survived as an anachronism in his age, but was still remembered, and at his funeral in Westminster Abbey 'all or the greatest part of the nobility and gentry then in the town' were present. Story has it that the intended monument to him was never erected, and that it was a visitor to the Abbey who, noticing the gravestone, gave a stone-cutter one and sixpence to carve the epitaph that has become famous: 'O rare Ben Jonson.'

'Energy is eternal delight.' Blake's formula often comes to mind as one reads the Elizabethans, and in none more than Ben Jonson. In the early comedies there is almost too much of it: a sense of overcrowding, of having too much to say. Later the energy lost nothing and the mastery over it increased. In no play do we feel this more infectiously than in *The Alchemist*.

The Alchemist is that remarkable thing, a work of art classically controlled yet striking one at all points as enjoying the freedoms of a spontaneous, fresh liveliness. So much of the rarity of Ben Jonson lies there. He was a scholar, who knew the dramatic laws and respected them. He applies them in this play; the action takes place in twenty-four hours and in, or just outside, a single house. He constructs his plot with formal perfection, each episode neatly dovetailed into the next, and he keeps the various plots going with the virtuosity of a juggler. But this is all at one with a sense of fun that has nothing dully academic about it, and a verbal energy that is entirely of its own period.

Finally there is the satisfaction of an entertainment that, in a much more serious way than, say, the comedies of Sheridan and Goldsmith, is directed by a mature moral and social consciousness. The hard, grasping energy of the age, the life that springs out of the dunghills of London's poverty, the outrage of a luxurious, cavalier self-indulgence among silly courtiers, and of a pale-faced power-seeking puritanism at the other extreme; all these are caught and condemned. This is one side of the play's morality. The other is more positive, less explicit and probably less expected. That is the joy in wit that the play expresses. Wit in the trio of rogues is a creative force. They create for Sir Mammon the *novo orbe*, the Eldorado of his hopes: this cobwebby London house has become for him a fantasy place of glamour and promise. The spell over his mind is the creation of this wit. They create too the characters of 'the cunning man', of 'Captain' Face and of 'Lungs', the alchemists' assistant. Dol creates the mathematical lady mad from overmuch study of Broughton's works. They are artists. As against this, Surly with his heavy scepticism and his passive, rather absurd impersonation of the Spanish Don has no real life to offer. Jonson's own creative joy is with his entertainers, and that is no doubt why he lets them off lightly at the end. Perhaps this is 'irresponsible' and inferior to the stern judgment at the end of *Volpone*. Yet in that play too there is a sense of a creative liveliness in Mosca and Volpone that comes near to redeeming them. Volpone joys not so much in 'the glad possession' as in 'the cunning purchase', and Mosca could skip out of his skin with the spring in his blood. In *The Alchemist* it is this confrontation that is finally brought to focus; a creative vitality that is precious even in criminals, against a heavy, delusive folly that is deadly even in the law-abiding and respectable. The zest and challenge of the play are in that.

TO THE LADY, MOST DESERVING HER NAME AND BLOOD: MARY, LADY WROTH[1]

Madame,

In the age of sacrifices, the truth of religion was not in the great-
ness and fat of the offerings, but in the devotion and zeal of the
sacrificers. Else what could a handful of gums have done in the
sight of a hecatomb? Or how might I appear at this altar, except
with those affections that no less love the light and witness, than 5
they have the conscience of your virtue? If what I offer bear an
acceptable odour and hold the first strength, it is your value of it,
which remembers where, when and to whom it was kindled. Otherwise, as the times are, there comes rarely forth that thing so full
of authority or example, but by assiduity and custom grows less 10
and loses. This, yet, safe in your judgment (which is a Sydney's),

1–3. *In the age of sacrifices*: an idea familiar from the Bible, but here deriving
from Seneca. A translation of *De Beneficiis* (i, vi, 2) goes: 'Not in the
greatest victories, however golden the spoils, is there honour to the gods,
but rather in pious and upright homage of the spirit.'

3. *a handful of gums*: gums from trees and shrubs used for burning as incense. A *hecatomb* was a religious sacrifice on a grand scale, involving, in its
literal sense, a hundred oxen. So Jonson's meaning is this: 'It was not the
size of the sacrifice that mattered in the old days; rather the spirit in which
it was made. If this had not been so, then a poor little offering, such as a
pinch of incense, would have stood no chance of pleasing the gods, as it
couldn't possibly compare with the grandeur of the great public ceremonies.'

The religious metaphor is carried into the next sentences. 'Similarly',
he argues, 'here am I offering the gift of this play to you, presenting it like
one who stands before an altar with a sacrifice, and hoping its sincerity will
ensure that it proves acceptable.'

5. *the light and witness*: as in Shakespeare's phrase 'the witness of a good
conscience' (*Merry Wives of Windsor* (IV, ii, 220)). *Conscience*, as it occurs
later in Jonson's sentence, means 'knowledge' or 'consciousness'. The
meaning, then, is this: 'I would not dare to offer you this play of mine if I
were not both a conscientious lover of truth, and a man fully aware of your
own goodness.'

10. *by assiduity*: 'by repetition' or 'frequency'. 'If I didn't have the double
guarantee of my good conscience and your good nature, I should have no
assurance that my work would survive: for we see nowadays that however
authoritative and exemplary a thing may be, it grows stale with repetition
and loses interest as it becomes increasingly familiar.'

[1] *Lady Mary Wroth*: a daughter of Robert Sidney, 1st Earl of Leicester
and brother of Sir Philip Sidney. Jonson mentioned her to Drummond as
'unworthily married on a jealous husband' (Sir Robert Wroth was a keen
sportsman, while Lady Mary patronised writers and wrote poetry herself).
She acted in one of Jonson's court entertainments, *The Masque of Blackness*,
given in 1605; and in 1621 she published *Urania*. Lord Denny complained
that in it 'she doth palpably and grossly play upon him and his late daughter
. . . besides many others she makes bold with'. She survived these conflicts
and is still heard of as late as 1640, three years after Jonson's death.

23

is forbidden to speak more, lest it talk or look like one of the ambitious faces of the time, who, the more they paint, are the less
themselves.

Your Ladyship's true honourer,   15
Ben. Jonson.

12. *forbidden to speak more*: 'This' means 'the present author'. So the sense of
    the last sentence is: 'I am confident of your good judgment and will not
    write any more, as otherwise I shall probably look like one of those self-
    interested folk who put on affected manners of speech and behaviour, and
    so are ever becoming less recognisable as their true selves.'

TO THE READER

If thou beest more, thou art an Understander, and then I trust thee. If thou art one that tak'st up, and but a Pretender, beware at what hands thou receiv'st thy commodity. For thou wert never more fair in the way to be cozened than in this age in poetry, especially in plays; wherein now the concupiscence of dances and 5 anticks so reigneth, as to run away from Nature and be afraid of her is the only point of art that tickles the spectators. But how out of purpose and place do I name art, when the professors are grown so obstinate condemners of it and presumers on their own naturals, as they are deriders of all diligence that way, and, by 10 simple mocking at the terms when they understand not the things, think to get off wittily with their ignorance. Nay, they are esteemed the more learned and sufficient for this, by the many, through their excellent vice of judgment. For they commend writers as they do fencers or wrestlers, who, if they come in 15 robustuously and put for it with a great deal of violence, are received for the braver fellows; when many times their own rudeness

4. *fair in the way to be cozened*: never more likely to be cheated.

5–6. *concupiscence of dances and anticks*: Jonson is deploring what he saw as indecorum in the contemporary theatre. Plays should not have to be garnished with dances and clownish knockabout in order to make them attractive to people who have no taste. Shakespeare's plays were sometimes given with these 'impurities' that Jonson is decrying. So the diary of a German traveller named Platter (see E. K. Chambers, *The Elizabethan Stage*, ii, 364–5) records a visit to what he calls the 'comedy' of *Julius Caesar*, at the end of which 'they danced according to their custom with extreme elegance'. It is even possible that Jonson is by implication criticising Shakespeare in this introduction. See Herford and Simpson. (Introduction to *The Alchemist*, p. 52)

9–10. *presumers on their own naturals*: Playwrights nowadays trust to their own native wit and do not bother to learn writing as an art. In addition to this, they will make fun of those who do take it seriously ('deriders of all diligence that way').

11. *mocking at the terms*: there is a kind of ignorant 'wit' that will gain cheap popularity by making fun of things intellectual. Any art has its 'terms', and the classical rules of construction and various devices of 'discovery', 'reversal of fortune' etc., all have their technical names, fair game for anyone who regarded them as so much pedantic jargon. Jonson says that people who scoff in this way do so to obtain a cheap laugh without really knowing what they are talking about.

14. *excellent*: exceptional (cf. *Antony and Cleopatra*: 'Excellent falsehood' (I, i, 40)).

17. *their own rudeness*: roughness. The display of brute massiveness and animal energy hides their want of technical knowledge, and a lack there will often prove their downfall, cf. Jonson's *Discoveries* (ll. 634–42) with the same comparison between playwrights and games-players, concluding: 'But in these things, the unskilful are naturally deceived, and judging wholly by the bulk, think rude things greater than polished, and scattered more

25

is the cause of their disgrace, and a little touch of their adversary gives all that boisterous force the foil. I deny not but that these men, who always seek to do more than enough, may sometime 20 happen on something that is good and great; but very seldom. And when it comes it doth not recompense the rest of their ill. It sticks out, perhaps, and is more eminent, because all is sordid and vile about it; as lights are more discerned in a thick darkness than a faint shadow. I speak not this out of a hope to do good on any 25 man against his will; for I know, if it were put to the question of theirs and mine, the worse would find more suffrages, because the most favour common errors. But I give thee this warning: that there is a great difference between those that, to gain the opinion of copy, utter all they can, however unfitly, and those that use 30 election and a mean. For it is only the disease of the unskilful to think rude things greater than polished, or scattered more numerous than composed.   33

numerous than composed': phrases used almost word for word in the last sentences of this introduction.

27. *more suffrages*: more votes or support.

29–30. *the opinion of copy*: the reputation of copiousness (of thinking quickly and writing fluently).

31. *election and a mean*: discrimination and moderation.

32–33. *scattered . . . than composed*: Ignorant people will find unorganised, easy-going writing more to their liking than a disciplined work of art. 'Numerous' probably has two meanings, one continuing the sense of 'copy' above (copious, abundant), the other having the literary sense of 'numbers' (verse that is pleasing to the ear, rhythmical and harmonious).

THE PERSONS OF THE PLAY

SUBTLE, The Alchemist.
FACE, The House-keeper.
DOL COMMON, Their Colleague.
DAPPER, A Clerk.
DRUGGER, A Tobacco-man.
LOVEWIT, Master of the house.
EPICURE MAMMON, A Knight.
SURLY, A Gamester.
TRIBULATION WHOLESOME, A Pastor of Amsterdam.
ANANIAS, A Deacon there.
KASTRIL, The Angry Boy.
DAME PLIANT, His Sister, A Widow.

Neighbours.
Officers.
Mutes.

THE SCENE

London.

THE ARGUMENT[1]

The sickness hot, a master quit, for fear,
His house in town, and left one servant there.
Ease him corrupted and gave means to know
A cheater and his punk, who, now brought low,
Leaving their narrow practice, were become   5
Cozeners at large; and only wanting some
House to set up, with him they here contract,
Each for a share, and all begin to act.
Much company they draw, and much abuse,
In casting figures, telling fortunes, news,   10
Selling of flies, flat bawdry, with the stone;
Till it, and they, and all in fume are gone.

1. *The sickness hot*: the plague, which afflicted London in those times; serious throughout 1609 and the latter part of 1610.
4. *his punk*: prostitute-girl friend. A common Elizabethan slang term, though not appearing in literature till about 1600 (O.E.D.).
6. *cozeners at large*: cheaters in a bolder, more extensive way of business.
10. *casting figures*: making horoscopes (cf. *Alchemist* (IV. iv): 'By erection of her figure, I guessed it').
11. *selling of flies*: a fly was a 'familiar', a demon supposed to be under a man's control. The Devil was believed to assume the form of flies.
flat bawdry: involves a bawdy secondary-meaning in the word 'stone'. The surface meaning is that all sorts of practices went on in this house with the finding of the philosopher's stone as their excuse. But 'stone' was also a slang word for 'testicle': hence references in *Henry IV Part 2* (III, ii, 329) and *Timon of Athens* (II, ii, 113–18) to the philosopher's 'two stones', and hence the punning joke here.
12. *in fume*: in vapour. Again a double meaning: (i) the alchemical experiment is supposed to fail, and everything is *in fumo* (see p. 121, l. 58); (ii) the characters, the actors, both vanish as though in a cloud of smoke, transitory, ephemeral creatures who pass before our gaze for a short spell of time and then are gone.

[1] *The Argument*: the plot. It was customary to introduce the play with a poem or a piece of dumb-show which would give an outline of the story (cf. the King's question about the play in *Hamlet*: 'Have you heard the argument? Is there no offence in't?' (III, ii, 221)). Jonson's poem is in the form of an acrostic, as in *Volpone*.

PROLOGUE

Fortune, that favours fools, these two short hours
  We wish away, both for your sakes and ours,
Judging spectators; and desire, in place,
  To th'author justice, to ourselves but grace.
Our scene is London, 'cause we would make known   5
  No country's mirth is better than our own.
No clime breeds better matter for your whore,
  Bawd, squire, impostor, many persons more,
Whose manners, now called humours, feed the stage,
  And which have still been subject for the rage   10
Or spleen of comic-writers. Though this pen
  Did never aim to grieve, but better men,
Howe'er, the age he lives in doth endure
  The vices that she breeds, above their cure.
But when the wholesome remedies are sweet,   15
  And, in their working, gain and profit meet,
He hopes to find no spirit so much diseased,
  But will, with such fair correctives, be pleased.
For here he doth not fear who can apply.
  If there be any that will sit so nigh   20
Unto the stream to look what it doth run,
  They shall find things they'd think, or wish, were done;
They are so natural follies, but so shown
  As even the doers may see, and yet not own.

1. *Fortune . . . we wish away*: For the success of his play, Jonson will trust the good judgment of his audience rather than appeal to mere good luck.
two short hours: Most plays of the time, including *The Alchemist*, take longer than this in performance. Several other prologues, however, make similar references (e.g. *Romeo and Juliet* and *Henry VIII*).
4. *ourselves*: the company. The Prologue would be spoken by one of the actors.
9. *manners, now called humours*: What the Restoration came to call the comedy of manners was then modishly called the comedy of humours. Jonson had set the fashion in his first two plays (*Every Man In his Humour* and *Every Man Out of his Humour*), where we see characters with their particular individuality stressed so that their 'humour' can be seen clearly. See Introduction p. 8. In this present Prologue Jonson may be noting that his term has 'caught on' well; also a little irritated that it has become public property, loosely understood and wrongly used.
18. *correctives*: stress on the first syllable.
23–24. *they are so natural follies*: 'The comedy is so lifelike that, watching it closely, you will think you are seeing life itself; yet the playwright has been truthful and even those who themselves indulge in such follies will recognise the accuracy of the picture without feeling themselves embarrassingly exposed by it.'

ACT I

Scene 1: *A room in Lovewit's house*

Enter FACE, *in a captain's uniform, with his sword drawn and*
SUBTLE *with a vial, quarrelling, and followed by* DOL COMMON

FACE   Believe't, I will!

SUBTLE   Thy worst! I fart at thee!

DOL   Ha' you your wits? Why gentlemen! for love—

FACE   Sirrah, I'll strip you—

SUBTLE   What to do? lick figs

Out at my—

FACE   Rogue, rogue, out of all your sleights!

DOL   Nay, look ye! Sovereign, general, are you madmen?   5

SUBTLE   Oh, let the wild sheep loose. I'll gum your silks

With good strong water, an you come.

DOL   Will you have

The neighbours hear you? Will you betray all?

Hark! I hear somebody.

FACE   Sirrah—

SUBTLE   I shall mar

All that the tailor has made if you approach.   10

FACE   You most notorious whelp! You insolent slave!

Dare you do this?

SUBTLE   Yes, faith: yes, faith.

FACE   Why! Who

Am I, my mongrel? Who am I?

1. *Thy worst!*: Do your worst!
3. *lick figs*: a reference to the story of Frederick Barbarossa dealing with
rebels in Rabelais' *Pantagruel*: 'Then the hangman, by his order, clasped a
fig into the mule's jimcrack, in the presence of the enslaved cits that were
brought into the middle of the great market-place, and proclaimed, in the
Emperor's name, with trumpets, that whatsoever of them would save his
own life should publicly pull the fig out with his teeth, and after that put
it in again in the very individual cranny whence he had drawed it without
using his hands; and that whoever refused to do this should presently
swing for it and die in his shoes' (Bk. IV, xlv, trans. 1653).
4. *out of all your sleights*: 'I'll strip you of all the trickeries with which you
protect yourself.'
5. *sovereign, general*: Dol habitually uses these inflated terms for her
confederates.
6. *let the wild sheep loose*: taking up the term 'madness', and meaning 'If you
have a sheep that has gone out of its mind, better let it rove rather than
enrage the rest of the flock'.
   gum your silks: Face is dressed in his Captain's uniform and Subtle
threatens to spoil his finery by throwing the chemicals in his vial at him
if he comes nearer.
10. *all that the tailor has made*: 'You won't be able to cut such a fine figure if
I make a mess of your uniform.' (Cf. the proverb 'The Taylor makes the
man').

SUBTLE   I'll tell you,
Since you know not your self—
FACE   Speak lower, rogue!
SUBTLE.   Yes. You were once (time's not long past) the good,   15
Honest, plain, livery-three-pound-thrum, that kept
Your master's worship's house here in the Friars
For the vacations—
FACE   Will you be so loud?
SUBTLE   Since, by my means, translated Suburb-Captain.
FACE   By your means, Doctor dog?
SUBTLE   Within man's memory   20
All this I speak of.
FACE   Why, I pray you, have I
Been countenanced by you? Or you by me?
Do but collect, sir, where I met you first.
SUBTLE   I do not hear well.
FACE   Not of this, I think it.
But I shall put you in mind, sir: at Pie Corner!   25
Taking your meal of steam in from cooks' stalls,
Where, like the father of hunger, you did walk
Piteously costive, with your pinch'd-horn nose,
And your complexion of the Roman wash,
Stuck full of black and melancholic worms,   30

16. *livery-three-pound-thrum*: instead of having the fine clothes he is now
    wearing, Face was once dressed in a poor servant's outfit. 'Thrum' is the
    loose ends of a warp, used for cheap materials. Three pounds would be the
    servant's annual wage. Subtle is taking him down a peg or two, reminding
    him also of the homely virtues ('good', 'honest', 'plain') which he can no
    longer claim as part of his reputation.

19. *translated Suburb-Captain*: not a genuine commission, but a title which he
    is known by locally, cf. *Henry IV* Part II (II, iv, 133) 'Captain [was] an
    excellent good word before it was ill-sorted: therefore captains had need
    look to't'. 'Translated' means 'promoted to'.

23. *collect*: recollect.

24. *I do not hear well*: he hears perfectly well but means 'I'm not listening to
    this—I'm deaf to anything you may say'.

25. *Pie Corner*: the approach to West Smithfield, a district that had gone
    down in respectability. There had been a famous inn there, but by Jonson's
    time it was divided into tenements.

26. *your meal of steam*: there were turnspits at Pie Corner, and if a person
    had no money he could at least treat himself to the smell of roasting meat
    or other food. This was the best that Subtle could do for himself in those
    days.

27. *father of hunger*: Herford and Simpson note two classical derivations
    here: Catullus (xxi) for the phrase itself, and Martial (I, xcii. 7–10) for other
    details. The lines from Martial include the idea of living 'on the mere
    smell of the black kitchen'.

28. *costive*: constipated.

29. *the Roman wash*: probably a preparation that acts as an antidote to
    venereal diseases. So Subtle's skin disorders have been treated with this
    and there is an allusion to the bad habits which have caused them.

Like powder-corns shot at the Artillery Yard.
SUBTLE   I wish you could advance your voice a little.
FACE   When you went pinned up in the several rags
You had raked and picked from dunghills before day,
Your feet in mouldy slippers for your kibes,   35
A felt of rug and a thin threaden cloak
That scarce would cover your no-buttocks—
SUBTLE   So, sir!
FACE   When all your alchemy and your algebra,
Your minerals, vegetals and animals,
Your conjuring, cozening, and your dozen of trades,   40
Could not relieve your corps with so much linen
Would make you tinder but to see a fire:
I ga' you countenance, credit for your coals,
Your stills, your glasses, your materials;
Built you a furnace, drew you customers,   45
Advanced all your black arts, lent you, beside,
A house to practise in—
SUBTLE   Your master's house!
FACE   Where you have studied the more thriving skill
Of bawdry since.
SUBTLE   Yes, in your master's house.
You and the rats here kept possession.   50
Make it not strange. I know you were one could keep
The buttery-hatch still locked, and save the chippings,

31. *powder-corns shot at the Artillery Yard*: The Artillery Garden in London
   was opened in 1610 for arms practice, so the allusion was a very topical
   one. 'Powder-corns' (or 'corn-powder') was gunpowder that had been
   'corned' or granulated.
32. *advance your voice*: 'I wish you would speak up.' Subtle is still pretending
   he can't hear these insults.
35. *kibes*: chilblains.
36. *felt of rug*: a 'felt' was a hat. 'Rug' is a kind of coarse woollen cloth, or
   frieze.
39. *vegetals*: vegetables, in the sense of a classification of one of the three
   main forms of existing objects.
40. *cozening*: cheating.
41–42. *relieve your corps*: 'You couldn't make enough money to buy yourself
   clothes that (if you tried to burn them) would keep a fire going for a
   minute.'
43. *countenance*: authority.
44. *stills*: alembic, or retort, used for distilling liquids.
48. *thriving skill of bawdry*: Subtle has turned Lovewit's house into a
   brothel. The profession of bawdy-house keeper is a busy and profitable
   one.
52–53. *the buttery-hatch still locked*: from the buttery-hatch of well-to-do
   houses food would be distributed to poor dependents. 'Chippings' were the
   bits of crust cut off as waste from the loaf; and 'dole-beer', like 'dole-
   bread' as the chippings were called, was also given out. Face, as butler,
   would be entrusted with these charitable offices, and, if unscrupulous,
   could keep the food or sell it for private profit.

Sell the dole-beer to aqua-vitae men,
The which, together with your Christmas vails,
At post-and-pair, your letting out of counters,   55
Made you a pretty stock, some twenty marks,
And gave you credit to converse with cobwebs,
Here, since your mistress' death hath broke up house.

FACE   You might talk softlier, rascal.

SUBTLE   No, you scarab,
I'll thunder you in pieces. I will teach you   60
How to beware to tempt a Fury again
That carries tempest in his hand and voice.

FACE   The place has made you valiant.

SUBTLE   No: your clothes.
Thou vermin! Have I ta'en thee out of dung,
So poor, so wretched, when no living thing   65
Would keep thee company, but a spider, or worse?
Raised thee from brooms and dust and watering-pots?
Sublimed thee and exalted thee and fixed thee
I' the third region called our state of grace?
Wrought thee to spirit, to quintessence, with pains   70
Would twice have won me the philosopher's work?
Put thee in words and fashion? Made thee fit
For more than ordinary fellowships?
Given thee thy oaths, thy quarrelling dimensions?

53. *aqua-vitae men*: distillers and sellers of spirits. Aqua-vitae was an
    alchemist's term for strong alcoholic spirits, popularly used for any sort of
    strong drink.
54. *Christmas vails*: 'Vails' means profits or tips: the money that
    would be thought of as legitimately going to the butler's box at Christmas
    time.
55. *post-and-pair*: a game. Each player had three cards, the best hand to have
    being three aces, then three kings, three queens etc. Face would reckon
    to do well out of this.
    letting out of counters: imitation coins used in gambling. The players would
    pay for the hire.
56. *twenty marks*: a mark was worth 13/4 or two-thirds of a pound.
59. *scarab*: a dung-beetle (Greek 'scarabos': a beetle).
61. *a Fury*: an avenging spirit sent to punish crime.
63. *No: your clothes*: 'It's the finery of your Captain's uniform that has
    infuriated me.'
69. *the third region*: the air was said to be divided into three regions. Subtle
    reckons that he has brought Face up from the lowest to the highest;
    sublimed him, in alchemists' terms, or raised him above a gross, earthy
    state.
71. *the philosopher's work*: 'I deserve to have won the philosopher's stone
    (the culmination of an alchemist's ambition) twice over.'
72. *put thee in words and fashion*: 'taught you fashionable speech and
    manners'.
74. *given thee thy oaths*: To cut a dash in society one needed to know the
    fashionable oaths (cf. Master Stephen in *Every Man in his Humour* im-
    pressed by Captain Bobadill).
    quarrelling dimensions: Later Kastril comes for instructions in how to

Thy rules to cheat at horse-race, cock-pit, cards,   75
Dice, or whatever gallant tincture else?
Made thee a second in mine own great art?
And have I this for thank? Do you rebel?
Do you fly out i' the projection?
Would you be gone now?

DOL (*coming between them*)   Gentlemen, what mean you?   80
Will you mar all?

SUBTLE   Slave, thou hadst had no name—

DOL   Will you undo yourselves with civil war?

SUBTLE   Never been known, past *equi clibanum*,
The heat of horse-dung, underground, in cellars,
Or an ale-house darker than deaf John's; been lost   85
To all mankind, but laundresses and tapsters,
Had not I been!

DOL   Do you know who hears you,
Sovereign?

FACE   Sirrah—

DOL   Nay, general, I thought you were civil—

FACE   I shall turn desperate if you grow thus loud.

SUBTLE   And hang thyself, I care not.

FACE   Hang thee, collier,   90
And all thy pots and pans, in picture I will,
Since thou hast moved me—

DOL (*aside*)   Oh, this'll o'erthrow all.

FACE   Write thee up bawd in Paul's; have all thy tricks
Of cozening with a hollow coal, dust, scrapings,
Searching for things lost, with a sieve and sheers,   95

quarrel. The art was concerned with style, and the avoidance of too
serious consequences.

76. *tincture*: literally 'colouring'; philosophically the infusion of a spiritual
quality into material things. Subtle feels he has coloured or infused Face
with a gallantry and style far beyond his upbringing.

79. *fly out i' the projection*: an alchemist's term again (projection: the final
phase in the process of transmutation), meaning here 'Are you trying to be
difficult just now when our schemes are coming nicely to boiling point?'

83. *past equi clibanum*: which Subtle then translates as the heat of horse-
dung.

85–86. *been lost to all mankind*: 'But for me, nobody would have known you
except low-class individuals like laundresses and bar-tenders.'

90. *Hang thee, collier*: perhaps a catch-phrase about this time (cf. 'Hang him,
foul collier': Sir Toby Belch of Satan *Twelfth Night* III, iv, 120). Colliers
were notorious for giving their customers false weight.

93. *write thee up bawd in Paul's*: business of various disreputable kinds was
carried on in St Paul's. Notices were posted; so, by advertising that Subtle
keeps a bawdy-house, Face could cause him embarrassment.

94. *cozening with a hollow coal*: a fairly familiar trick by Jonson's time (cf.
Canon Yeoman's Tale (160–4).

95. *with a sieve and sheers*: a device to catch a thief. Two people had to hold
the points of the shears in the wood of a sieve, then read a chapter of the
Bible, and ask St Peter or St Paul whether this man or that is the thief,

Erecting figures in your rows of houses,
And taking in of shadows with a glass
Told in red letters; and a face, cut for thee
Worse than Gamaliel Ratsey's.
DOL   Are you sound?
Ha' you your senses, masters?
FACE   I will have   100
A book, but barely reckoning thy impostures,
Shall prove a true philosopher's stone to printers.
SUBTLE   Away, you trencher-rascal!
FACE   Out, you dog-leach!
The vomit of all prisons—
DOL   Will you be
Your own destructions, gentlemen?
FACE   —still spewed out   105
For lying too heavy o' the basket.
SUBTLE   Cheater!
FACE   Bawd!
SUBTLE   Cowherd!
FACE   Conjurer!
SUBTLE   Cutpurse!
FACE   Witch!
DOL   Oh me!
We are ruined! Lost! Ha' you no more regard
To your reputations? Where's your judgment? 'Slight,
Have yet some care of me, o' your republic—   110
FACE   Away this brach! I'll bring thee, rogue, within
The statute of sorcery, *tricesimo tertio*,

naming all the people suspected. When the name of the actual thief is
mentioned, the sieve will suddenly turn around.
96. *figures in your rows of houses*: the houses were the signs of the zodiac,
and 'erecting figures' involved making diagrams of the planets' positions so
as to cast a person's horoscope.
97–98. *taking in of shadows with a glass*: the fortune-teller's crystal would
answer the questions put by means of the reflections or shadows seen in it.
The supernatural message would then be made to appear in impressive
antique script ('told in red letters') like the headings in old books.
99. *Gamaliel Ratsey*: a famous highwayman, executed in 1605, who wore a
frighteningly ugly mask.
sound: 'in your right mind'.
101–102. *A book . . . to printers*: 'I will write a book which by merely listing
your deceptions will prove a gold-mine to the printers.'
103. *trencher-rascal*: 'trencher-friend' and 'trencher-fly' meant a parasite (he
would consume as much of your goods as he was able to). Subtle's term
carries the same sense, intensified by 'rascal'.
dog-leach: a dog-doctor, who would make money out of the hurts sustained
by dogs in bull and bear-baiting.
106. *too heavy o' the basket*: taking more than his fair share of the food sent in
for the prisoners.
111. *brach*: bitch.
112. *the statute of sorcery*: 'None from henceforth shall use to multiply gold

Of Harry the Eight. Ay, and perhaps thy neck
Within a noose for laundring gold and barbing it.
DOL   You'll bring your head within a cockscomb, will you?   115
(*she snatches out* FACE'S *sword*) And you, sir, with your menstrue!
(*she breaks* SUBTLE'S *glass*) Gather it up!
      'Sdeath, you abominable pair of stinkards,
Leave off your barking and grow one again,
Or by the light that shines, I'll cut your throats.
I'll not be made a prey unto the Marshal,   120
For ne'er a snarling dog-bolt o' you both.
Ha' you together cozened all this while,
And all the world, and shall it now be said
You have made most courteous shift to cozen yourselves?
(*to* FACE) You will accuse him? You will bring him in   125
Within the statute? Who shall take your word?
A whoreson, upstart, apocryphal captain,
Whom not a Puritan in Blackfriars will trust
So much as for a feather! And you too (*to* SUBTLE)
Will give the cause, forsooth? You will insult   130
And claim a primacy in the divisions?
You must be chief? As if you only had
The powder to project with, and the work
Were not begun out of equality,
The venture tripartite, all things in common,   135
Without priority? 'Sdeath, you perpetual curs,
Fall to your couples again and cozen kindly
And heartily and lovingly as you should,
And lose not the beginning of a term,
Or, by this hand, I shall grow factious too   140
And take my part and quit you.

or silver, or use the craft of multiplication, and if any the same do, he shall
incur the pain of felony.'
116. *menstrue*: a solvent; any liquid agent by which a solid substance may be
dissolved.
120. *the Marshal*: Provost-Marshal, chief of police.
121. *dog-bolt*: a term of contempt; literally, some kind of bolt or blunt-
headed arrow. O.E.D. suggests 'perhaps one of little value that might be
shot at any dog'.
128–129. *Puritan in Blackfriars*: Blackfriars was the Puritan district in
London, and haberdashery, including feather-making, seems to have been
a principal occupation. Dol means that Face is so notorious that not even
these unworldly folk, simple souls as they are, would give him a penny-
worth on credit.
131. *a primacy in the divisions*: precedence, superiority.
133. *project*: 'projection' is the twelfth and last stage in the process of
alchemy.
139. *beginning of a term*: perhaps in the legal sense of the temporary possession of an estate. Dol, Face and Subtle are now in possession of Lovewit's
house, and Dol is pointing out how ridiculous it is to lose the opportunities
thus presented.
141. *take my part*: 'take the share that I am entitled to'.

FACE 'Tis his fault:
He ever murmurs and objects his pains,
And says the weight of all lies upon him.
SUBTLE Why, so it does.
DOL.   How does it? Do not we
Sustain our parts?
SUBTLE   Yes, but they are not equal.   145
DOL Why, if your part exceed today, I hope
Ours may tomorrow match it.
SUBTLE   Ay, they may.
DOL 'May', murmuring mastiff? Ay, and do! Death on me!
Help me to throttle him. (*she seizes* SUBTLE *by the throat*)
SUBTLE   Dorothy, Mistress Dorothy!
'Od's precious, I'll do anything! What do you mean?   150
DOL Because o' your fermentation and cibation?
SUBTLE Not I, by heaven—
DOL   Your Sol and Luna—help me. (*to*
                                                  FACE)
SUBTLE Would I were hanged then! I'll conform myself.
DOL Will you, sir? Do so, then, and quickly. Swear!
SUBTLE What should I swear?
DOL   To leave your faction, sir,   155
And labour kindly in the common work.
SUBTLE Let me not breathe if I meant aught beside.
I only used those speeches as a spur
To him.
DOL I hope we need no spurs, sir. Do we?
FACE 'Slid, prove today who shall shark best!
SUBTLE   Agreed!   160
DOL Yes, and work close, and friendly.
SUBTLE   'Slight, the knot
Shall grow the stronger for this breach, with me. (*they shake hands*)
DOL Why so, my good baboons! Shall we go make
A sort of sober, scurvy, precise neighbours,
That scarce have smiled twice sin' the King came in,   165
A feast of laughter at our follies? Rascals,

151. *fermentation and cibation*: the sixth and seventh stages in the conversion
of metals into gold. Dol is merely casting up the alchemist's jargon at
Subtle, saying 'Because you know all this nonsense, do you think you're
any better than the rest of us?'
152. *Sol and Luna*: The sun and the moon, alchemist's terms for gold and
silver.
160. *shark*: pick up a living by tricks and cheating.
162. *with me*: for my part (i.e. 'As far as I am concerned, this quarrel will
simply serve to make our friendship closer').
164. *precise*: puritanical.
166–167. *Rascals . . . see me ride*: 'These folk are rascals who would do anything for the pleasure of seeing me carted on hurdles through the streets
as a condemned whore.'

Would run themselves from breath to see me ride
Or you t'have but a hole to thrust your heads in,
For which you should pay ear-rent? No, agree!
And may Don Provost ride a-feasting long,   170
In his old velvet jerkin and stained scarfs,
My noble Sovereign and worthy General,
Ere we contribute a new crewel garter
To his most worsted worship.

SUBTLE   Royal Dol!
Spoken like Claridiana, and thyself!   175

FACE   For which, at supper thou shalt sit in triumph,
And not be styled 'Dol Common' but 'Dol Proper',
'Dol Singular'. The longest cut at night
Shall draw thee for his 'Dol Particular'! (*a bell rings*)

SUBTLE   Who's that? One rings! To the window, Dol. Pray
                                                     [heaven 180
(*exit* DOL) The master do not trouble us this quarter!

FACE   Oh, fear not him. While there dies one a week
O' the plague, he's safe from thinking toward London.
Beside, he's busy at his hop-yards now;
I had a letter from him. If he do,   185
He'll send such word for airing o' the house
As you shall have sufficient time to quit it.
Though we break up a fortnight, 'tis no matter.

SUBTLE   (*re-enter* DOL) Who is it, Dol?

DOL   A fine young quodling.

FACE   Oh, my lawyer's clerk, I lighted on last night   190
In Holborn at the Dagger. He would have
(I told you of him) a familiar
To rifle with at horses, and win cups.

DOL   Oh, let him in.

SUBTLE   Stay. Who shall do't?

FACE   Get you your robes on. I will meet him, as going out. 195

DOL   And what shall I do?

---

168. *a hole to thrust your heads in*: the pillory, and the likelihood of having
    your ears cut off as a further punishment.
170. *Don Provost*: the Provost-Marshal. *Don*: 'Sir', with an ironical flavour-
    ing through the association with the Spanish grandee.
173. *crewel garter*: 'crewel' was a thin worsted yarn. Also meaning the 'cruel
    garters' of the stocks: 'We are not going to be caught by the law, put in the
    stocks and fined, thus contributing to the Provost-Marshal's exchequer.'
174. *worsted*: worsted stockings despised by fops who wore silk.
175. *Claridiana*: a princess, spirited heroine of *The Mirror of Knighthood*.
189. *quodling*: codling, a rather elongated kind of apple, in several plays used
    to describe a callow youth.
191. *the Dagger*: an inn. Dagger ale and pies were famous.
192. *a familiar*: a familiar spirit, i.e. a spirit who is bound to the service of
    one man.
193. *rifle*: gamble.

FACE   Not be seen. Away! (*exit* DOL)
Seem you very reserved.
SUBTLE   Enough. (*exit*)
FACE (*aloud for* DAPPER *to hear*)   God b'w'you, sir.
I pray you let him know that I was here.
His name is Dapper. I would gladly have stayed but—

Scene 2

DAPPER (*off-stage*)   Captain, I am here.
FACE   Who's that? He's come, I think, Doctor.
(*enter* DAPPER) Good faith, sir, I was going away.
DAPPER   In truth,
I am very sorry, Captain.
FACE   But I thought
Sure I should meet you.
DAPPER   Ay, I am very glad.
I had a scurvy writ or two to make,   5
And I had lent my watch last night to one
That dines today at the sheriff's, and so was robbed
Of my pass-time. (*re-enter* SUBTLE *in his velvet cap and gown*)
Is this the cunning man?
FACE   This is his worship.
DAPPER   Is he a doctor?
FACE   Yes.
DAPPER   And ha' you broke with him, Captain?
FACE   Ay.
DAPPER   And how?   10
FACE   Faith, he does make the matter, sir, so dainty,
I know not what to say—
DAPPER   Not so, good Captain.
FACE   Would I were fairly rid on't, believe me.
DAPPER   Nay, now you grieve me, sir. Why should you wish so?
I dare assure you I'll not be ungrateful.   15
FACE   I cannot think you will, sir. But the law
Is such a thing—And then, he says, Read's matter

6. *lent my watch*: Dapper is trying to impress. A watch would be a valuable
   possession; that, and a friend dining at the Sheriff's, are mentioned to
   impress Face that he is dealing with a man of the world.
8. *pass-time*: time-piece.
10. *broke with him*: 'Have you broached the matter with him?'
11. *so dainty*: 'He is so fastidious, he treats it as a matter of such doubtful
    propriety.' Face is, of course, impressing on Dapper that they are doing
    him the greatest possible favour: this raises the price all round.
17. *Read's matter*: Dr Simon Read of Southwark, a dabbler in magic. One
    Toby Matthews had been robbed of £37 10s. and Dr Read undertook to
    raise spirits who would find the thief. The money was supposed to have
    been recovered 'by the aid of the said spirits and demons' and Dr Read,
    though brought to law in 1608, was pardoned. He probably had a lucky

Falling so lately—
DAPPER   Read? He was an ass,
And dealt, sir, with a fool.
FACE   It was a clerk, sir.
DAPPER A clerk?   20
FACE   Nay, hear me, sir, you know the law
Better, I think—
DAPPER   I should, sir, and the danger.
You know I showed the statute to you?
FACE   You did so.
DAPPER And will I tell, then? By this hand of flesh,
Would it might never write good court-hand more   25
If I discover. What do you think of me?
That I am a Chiaus?
FACE   What's that?
DAPPER   The Turk was here—
As one would say 'Do you think I am a Turk?'.
FACE   I'll tell the Doctor so.
DAPPER   Do, good sweet Captain.
FACE (to SUBTLE) Come, noble Doctor, pray thee, let's prevail. 30
This is the gentleman, and he is no Chiaus.
SUBTLE   Captain, I have returned you all my answer.
I would do much, sir, for your love. But this
I neither may nor can.
FACE   Tut, do not say so.
You deal now with a noble fellow, Doctor,   35
One that will thank you richly, and he's no Chiaus.
Let that, sir, move you.
SUBTLE   Pray you, forbear—
FACE He has four angels here—
SUBTLE   You do me wrong, good sir.
FACE Doctor, wherein? To tempt you with these spirits?
SUBTLE   To tempt my art and love, sir, to my peril.   40
'Fore heaven, I scarce can think you are my friend
That so would draw me to apparent danger.

escape, and Face can use his 'matter' (or case) to suggest that Subtle would
be taking a great risk in doing this service for Dapper.
26. *discover*: reveal, inform the police.
27. *Chiaus*: Dapper explains his reference by saying 'The Turk was here',
    i.e. 'The Turk who was in London recently'. In 1607, a Turk named
    Mustapha arrived in England saying that he was an ambassador from the
    Sultan. He called himself a Chaush (or messenger) and successfully
    imposed on the English authorities as he had done on the French. The
    Levant Company entertained him at a daily cost of £5, and he was later
    received at Windsor. So the meaning here is a combination of 'Turk'
    (= 'infidel') and 'cheat'.
38. *angels*: gold coins worth 10/- each.
42. *apparent*: obvious.

FACE   I draw you? A horse draw you, and a halter,
You and your flies together—
DAPPER   Nay, good Captain.
FACE   That know no difference of men.
SUBTLE   Good words, sir.   45
FACE   Good deeds, sir Doctor dog's-meat! 'Slight, I bring you
No cheating Clim o'the Cloughs, or Claribels,
That look as big as five-and-fifty and flush,
And spit out secrets like hot custard—
DAPPER   Captain—
FACE   Nor any melancholic under-scribe   50
Shall tell the vicar. But a special gentle,
That is the heir to forty marks a year,
Consorts with the small poets of the time,
Is the sole hope of his old grandmother,
That knows the law and writes you six fair hands,   55
Is a fine clerk and has his ciphering perfect,
Will take his oath o'the Greek Testament,
If need be in his pocket, and can court
His mistress out of Ovid.
DAPPER   Nay, dear Captain—
FACE   Did you not tell me so?
DAPPER   Yes, but I'd ha' you 60
Use master Doctor with some more respect.
FACE   Hang him, proud stag, with his broad velvet head!
But for your sake I'd choke ere I would change
An article of breath with such a puckfist—

45. *Good words, sir*: 'Be polite'.
47. *Clim o'the Cloughs*: an outlaw of earlier times.
     Claribels: a 'lewd' knight in *The Faery Queen*, Bk. IV. *five-and-fifty, and flush*: a winning hand at cards. A 'flush' was a hand of a single suit, beating even a sequence of fifty-five, which was itself strong. So: 'This man isn't some bold-faced braggart, who is as pleased with himself as if he had the most fantastic set of cards in his hand'.
51. *the vicar*: the vicar-general, who could act with the authority of the Bishop. i.e. 'He is no miserable little clerk who will carry tales to the authorities.'
52. *forty marks*: the mark was worth 13/4.
55. *six fair hands*: six kinds of handwriting (e.g. Italian, Roman, Chancery and Court hands, all different kinds of script).
56. *ciphering*: elementary arithmetic.
59. *out of Ovid*: Ovid's *Amores* and *Ars Amatoria* were the source of much elegant writing that passed as original offerings to the beloved. Face may mean: one, that Dapper has command of all the Ovidian elegance of diction; two, that he has learnt all Ovid had to teach about the art of making love and so is a highly skilled practitioner.
62. *broad velvet head*: The downy skin covering the stag's horn was called 'velvet'. Subtle will be wearing a doctor's velvet skull-cap.
64. *article of breath*: so much breath as is needed to pronounce a definite or indefinite article; or perhaps in the legal sense of 'article', a clause in a will

Come, let's be gone. (*going*)

SUBTLE   Pray you, let me speak with you.   65

DAPPER   His worship calls you, Captain.

FACE   I am sorry
I e'er embarked myself in such a business.

DAPPER   Nay, good sir. He did call you.

FACE   Will he take, then?

SUBTLE   First, hear me—

FACE   Not a syllable 'less you take.

SUBTLE   Pray ye, sir—

FACE   Upon no terms but an *assumpsit*.   70

SUBTLE   Your humour must be law. (*he takes the money*)

FACE   Why, now, sir, talk.
Now I dare hear you with mine honour. Speak.
So may this gentleman too.

SUBTLE (*he beckons to* FACE)   Why, sir—

FACE   No whispering!

SUBTLE   'Fore heaven, you do not apprehend the loss
You do yourself in this.

FACE   Wherein? For what?   75

SUBTLE   Marry, to be so importunate for one
That, when he has it, will undo you all.
He'll win up all the money i' the town!

FACE   How!

SUBTLE   Yes. And blow up gamester after gamester,
As they do crackers in a puppet-play.   80
If I do give him a familiar,
Give you him all you play for. Never set him,
For he will have it.

FACE   Y'are mistaken, Doctor.
Why, he does ask one but for cups and horses,
A rifling fly, none o' your great familiars.   85

DAPPER   Yes, Captain, I would have it, for all games.

SUBTLE   I told you so!

FACE   (*to* DAPPER) 'Slight, that's a new business!
I understood you a tame bird to fly
Twice in a term or so, on Friday nights,

or a statute, the sort of thing that Dapper as a clerk might spend much of
his time writing.
64. *puckfist*: braggart (the verb 'puck' meant to strike or butt).
68. *take*: 'do business'.
70. *an assumpsit*: a verbal promise to perform a certain service.
71. *humour*: whim.
80. *crackers in a puppet-play*: fireworks appear to have been a common
feature of the puppet-plays, cf. *Bartholomew Fair* (v. iii).
81. *familiar*: see p. 38 l. 192 (note).
82. *set*: 'never play against him, for he will win'.
85. *rifling fly*: a very minor spirit who would guide him to success when
playing dice ('rifling'), cf. *The Argument* l. 11. (note).

When you had left the office, for a nag   90
Of forty or fifty shillings.
DAPPER   Ay, 'tis true, sir,
But I do think, now, I shall leave the law,
And therefore—
FACE   Why, this changes quite the case!
Do you think that I dare move him?
DAPPER   If you please, sir,
All's one to him, I see.
FACE   What! For that money?   95
I cannot with my conscience. Nor should you
Make the request, methinks.
DAPPER   No, sir, I mean
To add consideration.
FACE   Why then, sir,
I'll try. (*to* SUBTLE) Say that it were for all games, Doctor?
SUBTLE   I say, then, not a mouth shall eat for him   100
At any ordinary, but on the score,
That is a gaming mouth, conceive me.
FACE   Indeed!
SUBTLE   He'll draw you all the treasure of the realm
If it be set him.
FACE   Speak you this from art?
SUBTLE   Ay, sir, and reason too: the ground of art.   105
He's o' the only best complexion
The Queen of Fairy loves.
FACE   What! is he?
SUBTLE   Peace!
He'll overhear you. Sir, should she but see him—
FACE   What?
SUBTLE   Do not you tell him.
FACE   Will he win at cards too?
SUBTLE   The spirits of dead Holland, living Isaac,   110
You'd swear were in him. Such a vigorous luck
As cannot be resisted. 'Slight, he'll put
Six o' your gallants to a cloak indeed.
FACE   A strange success that some man shall be born to!

101. *ordinary*: public eating-house. With this supernatural aid Dapper
   would be so successful that his sporting friends could claim credit with
   landlords all over London. Also a play on 'score' as a gaming term. Subtle
   is being very waggish: his 'conceive me' means 'You understand?' or
   'Get me?'.
104. *if it be set him*: if these are the stakes for which he is playing.
110. *dead Holland, living Isaac*: Holland was the surname of John and John
   Isaac, Dutch alchemists early in the 15th century. Their works were not
   published in England till 1600, and as a son is addressed, Jonson must
   have thought that one of the two was alive, the other dead.
113. *to a cloak*: i.e. 'strip them to the cloak; the last thing which a gallant
   parted with, as it served to conceal the loss of the rest' (Gifford).

SUBTLE   He hears you, man—

DAPPER   Sir, I'll not be ingrateful.   115

FACE   Faith, I have a confidence in his good nature.
You hear he says he will not be ingrateful.

SUBTLE   Why, as you please; my venture follows yours.

FACE   Troth, do it, Doctor! Think him trusty, and make him.
He may make us both happy in an hour;   120
Win some five thousand pound and send us two on't.

DAPPER   Believe it and I will, sir.

FACE   And you shall, sir.
You have heard all?

DAPPER   No, what was't? Nothing, I, sir.

FACE   Nothing?

DAPPER   A little, sir.

FACE   (takes him aside)   Well, a rare star
Reigned at your birth.

DAPPER   At mine, sir? No!

FACE   The Doctor   125
Swears that you are—

SUBTLE   Nay, Captain, you'll tell all now.

FACE   Allied to the Queen of Fairy.

DAPPER   Who? that I am?
Believe it, no such matter—

FACE   Yes, and that
You were born with a caul o' your head.

DAPPER   Who says so?

FACE   Come,
You know it well enough, though you dissemble it.   130

DAPPER   I'fac, I do not. You are mistaken.

FACE   How?
Swear by your fac? And in a thing so known
Unto the Doctor? How shall we, sir, trust you
I'the other matter? Can we ever think,
When you have won five, or six thousand pound,   135
You'll send us shares in't, by this rate?

DAPPER   By Jove, sir,
I'll win ten thousand pound and send you half.
I'fac's no oath.

SUBTLE   No, no, he did but jest.

---

118. *my venture follows yours*: 'My part in the affair begins only when you
have made your decision.'

129. *a caul o' your head*: A caul is a membrane that encloses the foetus in the
womb. A child is sometimes born with part of the caul on its head, proverbially taken as a sign of good luck.

132. *by your fac*: a variant on 'fay' ('faith'). 'By my fackins', 'feckins', 'feck',
and here 'fac', are all alternative forms of this very mild oath (as Dapper
protests later: 'I'fac's no oath').

FACE   Go to. Go, thank the Doctor. He's your friend
  To take it so.
DAPPER   I thank his worship.
FACE   So?   140
  Another angel.
DAPPER   Must I?
FACE   Must you? 'Slight,
  What else is thanks? Will you be trivial? (DAPPER *gives him
  the money*) Doctor,
  When must he come for his familiar?
DAPPER   Shall I not ha' it with me?
SUBTLE   Oh good sir!
  There must a world of ceremonies pass.   145
  You must be bathed and fumigated first.
  Besides, the Queen of Fairy does not rise
  Till it be noon.
FACE   Not if she danced tonight.
SUBTLE   And she must bless it.
FACE   Did you never see
  Her royal Grace yet?
DAPPER   Whom?
FACE   Your aunt of Fairy.   150
SUBTLE   Not since she kissed him in the cradle, Captain;
  I can resolve you that.
FACE   Well, see her Grace
  Whate'er it cost you, for a thing that I know!
  It will be somewhat hard to compass; but,
  However, see her. You are made, believe it,   155
  If you can see her. Her Grace is a lone woman,
  And very rich, and if she takes a fancy
  She will do strange things. See her, at any hand.
  'Slid, she may hap to leave you all she has!
  It is the Doctor's fear.
DAPPER   How will't be done, then?   160
FACE   Let me alone, take you no thought. Do you
  But say to me 'Captain, I'll see her Grace'.
DAPPER   Captain, I'll see her Grace.
FACE   Enough.
SUBTLE (*a knocking is heard*)   Who's there?
  (*calls*) Anon! (*to* FACE *aside*) Conduct him forth, by the back
                                                    [way.
  (*to* DAPPER) Sir, against one o'clock, prepare yourself.   165
  Till when, you must be fasting. Only, take

139. *Go to*: a common colloquialism, cf. 'Go on' or 'Get away with you'.
152. *I can resolve you that*: 'I can assure you on that point.'
153. *for a thing that I know*: 'there is something that I know' (i.e. that will
  make it worth your while, whatever the cost).

D

Three drops of vinegar in at your nose,
Two at your mouth, and one at either ear.
Then bathe your fingers' ends and wash your eyes
To sharpen your five senses, and cry 'Hum'   170
Thrice, and then 'Buz' as often, and then come. (*exit*)
FACE   Can you remember this?
DAPPER   I warrant you.
FACE   Well then, away. 'Tis but your bestowing
Some twenty nobles 'mong her Grace's servants;
And put on a clean shirt. You do not know   175
What grace her Grace may do you in clean linen.

Exeunt FACE *and* DAPPER

Scene 3

SUBTLE (*off stage*)   Come in! (Good wives, I pray you forbear
                                                          [me now.

Troth, I can do you no good till afternoon).
(*re-enters followed by* DRUGGER) What is your name,
say you? Abel Drugger?
DRUGGER   Yes, sir.
SUBTLE   A seller of tobacco?
DRUGGER   Yes, sir.
SUBTLE   Um . . .
Free of the grocers?
DRUGGER   Ay, an't please you.   5
SUBTLE   Well—your business, Abel?
DRUGGER   This, an't please your
                                                          [worship.

I am a young beginner and am building
Of a new shop, an't like your worship, just
At corner of a street. Here's the plot on't.
And I would know, by art, sir, of your worship,   10
Which way I should make my door, by necromancy,
And where my shelves, and which should be for boxes,
And which for pots. I would be glad to thrive, sir.
And I was wished to your worship by a gentleman,
One Captain Face, that says you know men's planets,   15
And their good angels and their bad.

---

167. *three drops of vinegar*: cf. 'Oh for three or four gallons of vinegar, to
    sharpen my wits! Revenge, vinegar revenge, vinegar and mustard
    revenge.' (*Every Man In his Humour* III, iii).
173. *'Tis but your bestowing*: 'It is just a simple matter: all you have to do is
    . . .' A noble was a coin worth 6/8.
1. *forbear me now*: 'Show some forbearance and don't trouble me for the
    present.' Subtle is talking to thin air, but it is to impress upon Drugger or
    anyone else that the establishment boasts an extensive clientele.
5. *free of the grocers*: 'You are a Freeman of the Company of Grocers?'
    Grocers sold tobacco, as did inn-keepers and apothecaries.

SUBTLE   I do,
If I do see 'em—

Re-enter FACE

FACE   What! My honest Abel?
Thou'rt well met here!
DRUGGER   Troth, sir, I was speaking,
Just as your worship came here, of your worship.
I pray you, speak for me to master Doctor.   20
FACE   He shall do anything. Doctor, do you hear?
This is my friend Abel, an honest fellow.
He lets me have good tobacco, and he does not
Sophisticate it with sack-lees or oil,
Nor washes it in muscadel and grains,   25
Nor buries it in gravel under ground,
Wrapped up in greasy leather or pissed clouts,
But keeps it in fine lily-pots, that opened
Smell like conserve of roses or French beans.
He has his maple block, his silver tongs,   30
Winchester pipes, and fire of juniper.
A neat, spruce-honest fellow, and no goldsmith.
SUBTLE   He's a fortunate fellow, that I am sure on—
FACE   Already, sir, have you found it? Lo thee, Abel!
SUBTLE   And in right way toward riches—
FACE   Sir!
SUBTLE   This summer   35
He will be of the clothing of his Company,
And next spring called to the scarlet. Spend what he can.
FACE   What, and so little beard?
SUBTLE   Sir, you must think
He may have a receipt to make hair come.

24. *sophisticate it*: adulterate it. Sometimes, when tobacco had lost strength,
    sellers would mix spices, wine or soil with it. 'Sack-lees': the sediment of
    the white wine called sack.
25. *muscadel*: a strong, sweet wine made from muscadine, a grape flavoured
    with musk.
27. *clouts*: pieces of cloth or clothing.
30. *maple block*: for shredding the tobacco leaf.
31. *fire of juniper*: at which customers could light their pipes.
32. *no goldsmith*: goldsmiths were also money-lenders. Face protests that
    Drugger is a well-turned-out, honest citizen and no usurer.
36. *the clothing of his Company*: He will be a livery-man in the Company of
    the Grocers (i.e. he will be promoted from freeman to be a member of this
    liveried Company).
37. *scarlet*: become sheriff of the City.
38. *so little beard*: meaning 'and at such an early age?', a rather sly, amused
    allusion to Drugger's awkward boyishness.
39. *receipt*: recipe, prescription.

But he'll be wise, preserve his youth, and fine for't.   40
His fortune looks for him another way.
FACE   'Slid, Doctor, how canst thou know this so soon?
I am amused at that!
SUBTLE   By a rule, Captain,
In metoposcopy, which I do work by:
A certain star i' the forehead which you see not.   45
Your chestnut or your olive-coloured face
Does never fail, and your long ear doth promise.
I knew't by certain spots, too, in his teeth,
And on the nail of his mercurial finger.
FACE   Which finger's that?   50
SUBTLE   His little finger.
Look. You were born upon a Wednesday?
DRUGGER   Yes indeed, sir.
SUBTLE   The thumb, in chiromancy, we give Venus,
The fore-finger to Jove, the midst to Saturn,
The ring to Sol, the least to Mercury,
Who was the lord, sir, of his horoscope,   55
His house of life being Libra, which fore-showed
He should be a merchant and should trade with balance.
FACE   Why, this is strange! Is't not, honest Nab?
SUBTLE   There is a ship now, coming from Ormus,
That shall yield him such a commodity   60
Of drugs—(*pointing to* DRUGGER'S *plan of the shop*)
This is the west, and this the south?
DRUGGER   Yes, sir.
SUBTLE   And those are your two sides?
DRUGGER   Ay, sir.
SUBTLE   Make me your door, then, south; your broad side,
                                                          [west;
And on the east side of your shop, aloft,

40. *fine for't*: The duties of sheriff were onerous, and on payment of a fine
   one could refuse the honour of undertaking them.
44. *metoposcopy*: literally the observing of the forehead. The metoposcopist
   claimed to read a person's fortune by studying his face and forehead.
52. *chiromancy*: palmistry, the art of telling fortunes from the hand.
55. *horoscope*: literally an observation of hours. At the hour of a person's
   birth the heavenly bodies are at a particular point in the sky, with certain
   of them 'in the ascendant'. These would then be the predominant in-
   fluences in the person's life, and each planet was reckoned to have its own
   character. In the astrologer's chart were twelve 'houses' ruled over by the
   planets. Subtle claims that Mercury was dominant at Drugger's birth; and
   this gives him special business ability and assurance of success. In fact, if
   the 'house of Life' was under Libra, then the ruling planet would have been
   Venus; but this is not what Drugger would want to learn, and so Subtle
   tells him a tale, on the principle that nothing succeeds like a success-story.
59. *Ormus*: Ormuz or Hormuz, a trading centre at the entrance to the Persian Gulf.

Write 'Mathlai', 'Tarmiel' and 'Baraborat';   65
Upon the north part, 'Rael', 'Velel', 'Thiel'.
They are the names of those Mercurial spirits
That do fright flies from boxes.
DRUGGER   Yes, sir.
SUBTLE   And,
Beneath your threshold, bury me a loadstone
To draw in gallants that wear spurs. The rest   70
They'll seem to follow.
FACE   That's a secret, Nab!
SUBTLE And, on your stall, a puppet, with a vice,
And a court-fucus, to call city-dames.
You shall deal much with minerals.
DRUGGER   Sir, I have
At home already—
SUBTLE   Ay, I know. You have arsenic,   75
Vitriol, sal-tartar, argaile, alkali,
Cinoper: I know all. This fellow, Captain,
Will come in time to be a great distiller,
And give a say (I will not say directly,
But very fair) at the Philosopher's Stone.   80
FACE Why, how now, Abel! Is this true?
DRUGGER (aside to FACE)   Good Captain,
What must I give?
FACE   Nay, I'll not counsel thee.
Thou hear'st what wealth (he says, spend what thou canst)
Th'art like to come to.
DRUGGER   I would gi' him a crown.
FACE A crown! And toward such a fortune? Heart,   85
Thou shalt rather gi' him thy shop! No gold about thee?
DRUGGER Yes, I have a portugue I ha' kept this half year.
FACE Out on thee, Nab! 'Slight, there was such an offer—

65. *Mathlai etc.,*: The mystic names come from a text-book of the occult,
    Heptameron, seu Elementa magica Pretri de Abano philosophi, published
    about 1567.
69. *loadstone*: magnet.
72. *puppet, with a vice*: The 'vice' was the apparatus which moved the eyes
    and lips of the puppet. This would be a good device to attract attention.
73. *court-fucus*: a cosmetic as used at court.
76. *vitriol*: sulphuric acid.
    sal-tartar: carbonate of potash.
    argail: argol, tartar deposited from wine and remaining on the sides of the
    cask.
    alkali: soda-ash.
77. *cinoper*: cinnabar, originally the most important ore of mercury, a
    crystalline form of mercuric sulphide.
84. *crown*: worth 5/-, coined first by Henry VIII as 'the Crown of the Rose'
    in 1526.
87. *a portugue*: a Portuguese gold piece. Its value varied from £3 5s. to
    £4 10s.

Shalt keep't no longer. I'll gi' it him for thee.
Doctor, Nab prays your worship to drink this, and swears   90
He will appear more grateful as your skill
Does raise him in the world.
DRUGGER   I would entreat
Another favour of his worship.
FACE   What is't, Nab?
DRUGGER   But to look over, sir, my almanack,
And cross out my ill-days that I may neither   95
Bargain nor trust upon them.
FACE   That he shall, Nab.
Leave it: it shall be done 'gainst afternoon.
SUBTLE   And a direction for his shelves.
FACE   Now, Nab?
Art thou well pleased, Nab?
DRUGGER   Thank, sir, both your worships.
FACE   Away!

Exit DRUGGER

(*to* SUBTLE) Why now, you smoky persecutor of nature!   100
Now, do you see that something's to be done
Beside your beech-coal and your corsive waters,
Your crosslets, crucibles and cucurbites?
You must have stuff brought home to you to work on.
And yet you think I am at no expense   105
In searching out these veins, then following 'em,
Then trying 'em out! 'Fore God, my intelligence
Costs me more money than my share oft comes to
In these rare works.
SUBTLE   You are pleasant, sir.

Re-enter DOL
                                    How now?
What says my dainty Dolkin?
DOL   Yonder fish-wife   110
Will not away. And there's your giantess,
The bawd of Lambeth.
SUBTLE   Heart, I cannot speak with 'em.
DOL   Not afore night, I have told 'em in a voice
Thorough the trunk, like one of your familiars.

100. *persecutor of nature*: a phrase used for an alchemist in Earle's *Micro-*
      cosmographie (1628).
102. *beech-coal*: charcoal made from beech-wood.
      corsive: corrosive.
103. *crosslets*: melting pots, a kind of crucible.
      cucurbites: a kind of retort, shaped like a gourd.
106. *these veins*: Face brings the 'customers' in. 'These veins' are the sources
      of profit waiting to be tapped.
114. *trunk*: speaking-tube.

But I have spied Sir Epicure Mammon—
SUBTLE   Where?   115
DOL   Coming along at far end of the lane,
Slow of his feet but earnest of his tongue
To one that's with him.
SUBTLE   Face, go you and shift.

Exit FACE

Dol, you must presently make ready too.
DOL   Why, what's the matter?
SUBTLE   Oh, I did look for him   120
With the sun's rising! Marvel he could sleep!
This is the day I am to perfect for him
The magisterium, our great work, the stone,
And yield it, made, into his hands: of which
He has, this month, talked as he were possessed.   125
And now he's dealing pieces on't away.
Methinks I see him entering ordinaries,
Dispensing for the pox; and plaguy-houses,
Reaching his dose; walking Moorfields for lepers;
And offering citizens' wives pomander-bracelets,   130
As his preservative, made of the elixir;
Searching the spittle to make old bawds young;
And the highways for beggars to make rich.
I see no end of his labours. He will make
Nature ashamed of her long sleep, when art,   135
Who's but a stepdame, shall do more than she
In her best love to mankind ever could.
If his dream last, he'll turn the age to gold.

Exeunt

123. *magisterium*: the Philosopher's Stone (literally 'mastery', which the stone was supposed to secure).
126. *dealing pieces on't away*: dispensing favours like a prince.
129. *Moorfields*: The stone was supposed to work medical as well as financial marvels. Moorfields was outside the City boundaries, and lepers, forbidden entry to the City, could beg there. Subtle sees Sir Epicure imagining himself tramping about to cure leprosy with his new godlike powers.
130. *pomander-bracelets*: Pomander was a mixture of aromatic substances said to be a preservative against infection in times of plague. A pomander chain or bracelet was the form in which it was carried.
132. *the spittle*: spital, or hospital, where the inmates would include those who ran bawdy houses and caught their diseases there.

ACT II

Scene 1: An outer room in Lovewit's house

Enter SIR EPICURE MAMMON *and* SURLY

MAMMON Come on, sir. Now you set your foot on shore
In *Novo Orbe*. Here's the rich Peru:
And there within, sir, are the golden mines,
Great Solomon's Ophir! He was sailing to't
Three years, but we have reached it in ten months.   5
This is the day wherein to all my friends
I will pronounce the happy word 'Be rich!'.
This day you shall be *Spectatissimi*.
You shall no more deal with the hollow die,
Or the frail card. No more be at charge of keeping   10
The livery-punk for the young heir, that must
Seal, at all hours, in his shirt. No more,
If he deny, ha' him beaten to't, as he is
That brings him the commodity. No more
Shall thirst of satin or the covetous hunger   15
Of velvet entrails for a rude-spun cloak
To be displayed at Madam Augusta's, make
The sons of sword and hazard fall before
The golden calf and on their knees, whole nights,
Commit idolatry with wine and trumpets,   20
Or go a-feasting after drum and ensign.
No more of this. You shall start up young Viceroys,
And have your punks and punketees, my Surly.
And unto thee I speak it first: 'Be rich!'.
(*calling*) Where is my Subtle there? Within, ho!   25

2. *Novo Orbe*: the new world. Lovewit's house is the world of great discovery for Mammon.

4. *Solomon's Ophir*: it was believed that Solomon's great wealth derived from his possession of the Stone. Ophir, probably in South Arabia or in Ethiopia, was the region to which his ships sailed in search of riches, and it was here, so legend had it, that he used the Stone to make gold. The courtiers at Jerusalem were not to be trusted with the secret, so the work was done in this distant country.

5. *three years*: 'For the King had at sea a navy of Tharshish with the navy of Hiram: once in three years came the navy of Tharshish, bringing gold, and silver, ivory, and apes, and peacocks' (I Kings x. 22).

8. *Spectatissimi*: 'most respected', i.e. very important citizens.

9. *hollow die*: a loaded dice ('die' an old form of the word).

10. *frail card*: a marked card for cheating.

11. *livery-punk*: a woman who would exercise her charms and make her gullible lover sign away his future in the heat of passion. 'Commodity' refers to the worthless goods tricksters would foist on a borrower instead of ready cash.

FACE (*within*)   Sir. He'll come to you by and by.
MAMMON   That's his fire-drake,
His lungs, his Zephyrus, he that puffs his coals
Till he firk nature up in her own centre.
You are not faithful, sir. This night I'll change
All that is metal in my house to gold.   30
And early in the morning will I send
To all the plumbers and the pewterers,
And buy their tin and lead up, and to Lothbury
For all the copper.
SURLY   What, and turn that too?
MAMMON   Yes, and I'll purchase Devonshire and Cornwall   35
And make them perfect Indies! You admire now?
SURLY   No, faith.
MAMMON   But when you see th'effects of the great medicine,
Of which one part projected on a hundred
Of Mercury or Venus or the Moon,
Shall turn it to as many of the Sun,   40
Nay, to a thousand, so *ad infinitum*.
You will believe me.
SURLY   Yes, when I see't I will.
But if my eyes do cozen me so (and I
Giving 'em no occasion), sure I'll have
A whore shall piss 'em out next day.
MAMMON   Ha! Why?   45
Do you think I fable with you? I assure you,
He that has once the flower of the sun,
The perfect ruby, which we call elixir,
Not only can do that, but by its virtue
Can confer honour, love, respect, long life,   50

26. *fire-drake*: the alchemist's assistant, one of whose main jobs would be to
    stoke the fire and see that it was kept going (like a human bellows—hence
    'Lungs', Mammon's name for Face). Holmyard mentions the nickname
    'souffleur' or 'puffer' for these people.
28. *firk*: stir.
29. *not faithful*: lacking in faith.
33. *Lothbury*: a street not far from Old Jewry. 'This street is possessed for
    the most part by founders, that cast candlesticks, chafing-dishes, spice
    mortars, and such-like copper or latten works, and do afterward turn them
    with the foot, and not with the wheel, to make them smooth and bright
    with turning and scrating, as some do term it, making a loathsome noise to
    the bypassers that have not been used to the like, and therefore by them
    disdainfully called Lothburie'. (Stow's *Survey of London*, 1598.)
36. *admire*: marvel, wonder, are impressed.
38. *projected on a hundred*: cf. *Canon Yeoman's Tale*:

>   The bodies sevene eek, lo! hem heer anoon.
>   Sol gold is, and Luna silver we threpe,
>   Mars yren, Mercurie quik-silver we clepe,
>   Saturnus leed, and Jupiter is tin,
>   And Venus copper, by my fader kin.   (272–6)

Give safety, valour, yea and victory,
To whom he will. In eight and twenty days
I'll make an old man of fourscore a child.

SURLY   No doubt; he's that already.

MAMMON   Nay, I mean
Restore his years, renew him, like an eagle,   55
To the fifth age; make him get sons and daughters,
Young giants; as our philosophers have done
(The ancient patriarchs afore the flood)
But taking once a week on a knife's point
The quantity of a grain of mustard of it: 60
Become stout Marses and beget young Cupids.

SURLY   The decayed vestals of Pict-hatch would thank you
That keep the fire alive there.

MAMMON   'Tis the secret
Of nature, naturized 'gainst all infections,
Cures all diseases, coming of all causes,   65
A month's grief in a day; a year's in twelve;
And of what age soever in a month,
Past all the doses of your drugging doctors.
I'll undertake withal to fright the plague
Out o' the kingdom in three months.

SURLY   And I'll   70
Be bound the players shall sing your praises then
Without their poets.

MAMMON   Sir, I'll do't. Meantime
I'll give away so much unto my man
Shall serve th'whole city with preservative,
Weekly, each house his dose, and at the rate—   75

SURLY   As he that built the water-work does with water?

MAMMON   You are incredulous.

SURLY   Faith, I have a humour

58. *ancient patriarchs*: Noah was said to be 600 years old at the time of the
   flood, his longevity being due to his knowledge of the secrets of alchemy.
62. *vestals of Pict-hatch*: a famous brothel; 'Vestals' is ironical. Surly means
   that Mammon's proposed gift of renewed potency to old men will earn him
   the gratitude of all the old baggages of London.
64. *nature, naturized*: jargon Sir Mammon has picked up from his dealings
   with bogus scholasticism. Naturized means 'endowed with a specific
   nature'.
71. *the players*: the actors, who had to close their theatres when the plague
   was severe, as in 1610 when *The Alchemist* was written.
76. *the water-work*: lead water-pipes serving houses with Thames water had
   been introduced in London by Peter Morris, a Dutchman, in 1582. Surly,
   still pulling Mammon's leg, says that no doubt he will arrange for his
   plague-preservative to be piped into houses by an arrangement like this
   still fairly recent and rather marvellous feat of engineering.
77. *have a humour*: 'It is a characteristic of mine that I'm not keen to be made
   a fool of. I'm not one of the things your Stone can work a major trans-
   formation upon.'

I would not willingly be gulled. Your Stone
Cannot transmute me.
MAMMON   Pertinax, my Surly,
Will you believe antiquity? Records?   80
I'll show you a book where Moses and his sister
And Solomon have written of the art.
Ay, and a treatise penned by Adam.
SURLY   How!
MAMMON   O' the Philosopher's Stone, and in High Dutch.
SURLY   Did Adam write, sir, in High Dutch?
MAMMON   He did: 85
Which proves it was the primitive tongue.
SURLY   What paper?
MAMMON   On cedar board.
SURLY   Oh, that indeed, they say,
Will last 'gainst worms.
MAMMON   'Tis like your Irish wood
'Gainst cobwebs. I have a piece of Jason's fleece, too,
Which was no other than a book of alchemy,   90
Writ in large sheep-skin, a good, fat ram-vellum.
Such was Pythagoras' thigh, Pandora's tub,
And all that fable of Medea's charms
The manner of our work: the bulls, our furnace
Still breathing fire; our argent-vive, the dragon;   95
The dragon's teeth, mercury sublimate,

---

81. *Moses*: Moses was supposed to have made the 'Red Elixir' and to him
and Miriam, his sister, were attributed various alchemical writings.
82. *Solomon*: 'the *Song of Solomon* was supposed to be an alchemical treatise
couched in veiled language' (Holmyard).
83. *Adam*: 'An extensive list of Adam's literary efforts, Noah's speeches
etc., is given in J. A. Fabricius' *Codex Pseudepigraphus Veteris Testamenti*,
1713'. (Herford and Simpson).
86. *the primitive tongue*: Mammon claims that High Dutch was the first
language in the world, cf. *A Restitution of Decayed Intelligence*, 1605, by R.
Verstegen, in which a physician is quoted as having persuaded the Regent
of the Netherlands that German was 'the first and most ancient language of
the world; yea the same that Adam spake in Paradise'. (Herford and
Simpson.)
88. *Irish wood*: It was believed that spiders would not make their webs on
Irish timbers, and this was ascribed to the special power of St. Patrick.
89. *Jason's fleece*: The golden fleece of a ram on which a notable escape had
been made was hung up in a grove at the south-eastern end of the Black
Sea, and guarded by a sleepless dragon. Alchemists believed that the real
value of the fleece (which Jason and the Argonauts captured), was that it
contained a parchment holding the secrets of alchemy.
92. *Pythagoras' thigh*: cf. 'World-famous, golden-thighed Pythagoras'
(*Among School-Children*, Yeats).
Pandora's Tub: presumably the jar or box given to Pandora by Zeus and
containing every evil known to man.
93. *Medea's charms*: Medea, daughter of Aetes of Colchis, was a famous
sorceress of classical mythology.

That keeps the whiteness, hardness and the biting.
And they are gathered into Jason's helm,
(Th' alembic) and then sowed in Mars's field,
And thence, sublimed so often, till they are fixed.   100
Both this, th'Hesperian garden, Cadmus' story,
Jove's shower, the boon of Midas, Argus' eyes,
Boccace's Demagorgon, thousands more:
All abstract riddles of our Stone.

Scene 2

Enter FACE *dressed as a servant*

                                                  How now?
Do we succeed? Is our day come? And holds it?
FACE   The evening will set red upon you, sir.
You have colour for it: crimson. The red ferment
Has done his office. Three hours hence, prepare you
To see projection.
MAMMON   Pertinax, my Surly,   5
Again I say to thee, aloud, 'Be rich!'.
This day thou shalt have ingots, and tomorrow
Give lords th'affront. Is it, my Zephyrus, right?
Blushes the bolt's head?
FACE   Like a wench with child, sir,
That were but now discovered to her master.   10
MAMMON   Excellent witty Lungs! My only care is
Where to get stuff enough now to project on.
This town will not half serve me.
FACE   No, sir? Buy
The covering o' the churches.
MAMMON   That's true.
FACE   Yes,
Let 'em stand bare, as do their auditory.   15
Or cap 'em new with shingles.

101. *Hesperian garden*: where the golden apples grew.
    Cadmus: who, in one version of the story, killed the dragon and sowed its
    teeth.
102. *Jove's shower*: Jove visited Danaë in a shower of gold.
    Midas: at whose touch everything changed to gold.
    Argus' eyes: the hundred-eyed giant set to guard Io.
103. *Boccace's Demagorgon*: Boccaccio wrote of these things in *De Genealogia
    Deorum*. Demagorgon, clothed in green, was 'the parent of all things'.
5. *projection*: the completion of the whole alchemical process, the twelfth
    stage at the end of which the Stone would be made.
7. *ingots*: bars of gold and silver.
8. *lords th'affront*: 'be as rude as you like to whoever you like.'
    my Zephyrus: because Face, 'Lungs', blows on the fire of the furnace out
    of which the Stone is to come.
9. *the bolt's head*: a globular flask with a long cylindrical neck. The liquor
    inside it would be red and glowing, therefore 'blushing'.

MAMMON   No: good thatch.
Thatch will lie light upon the rafters, Lungs.
Lungs, I will manumit thee from the furnace.
I will restore thee thy complexion, Puff,
Lost in the embers, and repair this brain,   20
Hurt wi' the fume o' the metals.
FACE   I have blown, sir,
Hard for your worship, thrown by many a coal
When 'twas not beech, weighed those I put in, just,
To keep your heat still even. These bleared eyes
Have waked to read your several colours, sir,   25
Of the pale citron, the green lion, the crow,
The peacock's tail, the plumed swan.
MAMMON   And, lastly,
Thou hast descried the flower, the *sanguis agni*?
FACE   Yes, sir.
MAMMON   Where's master?
FACE   At's prayers, sir, he;
Good man, he's doing his devotions   30
For the success.
MAMMON   Lungs, I will set a period
To all thy labours. Thou shalt be the master
Of my Seraglio.
FACE   Good, sir.
MAMMON   But, do you hear,
I'll geld you, Lungs.
FACE   Yes, sir.

---

15. *their auditory*: As the men of the congregation stand without hats in
   church, so the churches themselves should stand roofless (Mammon
   having taken all the lead for turning into gold).
16. *shingles*: give them a wooden roof. 'Shingles' were pieces of wood used
   as tiles for the roof.
18. *manumit*: to free a slave.
19. *restore . . . complexion*: cf. *Canon Yeoman's Tale*:

> 'Now', quod our host, 'yit lat me talke to the;
> Why artow so discoloured of thy face?'
> 'Peter!' quod he, 'god yeve it harde grace,
> I am so used in the fyr to blowe,
> That it hath chaunged my colour, I trowe.'
>   (Prologue 110–114)

22. *many of coal . . . not beech*: cf. *Canon Yeoman's Tale*:

> 'Because our fyr ne was nat maad of beech,
> This is the cause, and other noon, so theech!'
>   (375–6)

This is offered as a well-informed opinion on the cause of failure in an
alchemical endeavour.
24. *bleared*: grown tired-eyed, dull, filmy.
25. *several colours*: cf. Introduction p. 5.
31. *set a period*: put an end to (as a full-stop, 'period', closes a sentence).

MAMMON   For I do mean
  To have a list of wives and concubines   35
  Equal with Solomon, who had the Stone
  Alike with me. And I will make me a back
  With the elixir, that shall be as tough
  As Hercules, to encounter fifty a night.
  Th'art sure thou saw'st it blood?
FACE   Both blood and spirit, sir.   40
MAMMON   I will have all my beds blown up, not stuffed;
  Down is too hard. And then, mine oval room
  Filled with such pictures as Tiberius took
  From Elephantis, and dull Aretine
  But coldly imitated. Then my glasses,   45
  Cut in more subtle angles, to disperse
  And multiply the figures as I walk
  Naked between my succubae. My mists
  I'll have of perfume, vapoured 'bout the room,
  To lose ourselves in; and my baths like pits   50
  To fall into, from whence we will come forth
  And roll us dry in gossamer and roses.
  (Is it arrived at ruby?)—Where I spy
  A wealthy citizen or rich lawyer
  Have a sublimed pure wife, unto that fellow   55
  I'll send a thousand pound, to be my cuckold.
FACE   And I shall carry it?
MAMMON   No. I'll ha' no bawds,
  But fathers and mothers. They will do it best,
  Best of all others. And my flatterers
  Shall be the pure and gravest of divines,   60
  That I can get for money. My mere fools
  Eloquent burgesses, and then my poets,
  The same that writ so subtly of the fart,

36. *Solomon*: see p. 55. l. 82 notes. The elixir was also supposed to increase
    sexual potency.
43. *Tiberius*: 'A number of small rooms [at Tiberius' palace at Capri] were
    furnished with the most indecent pictures and statuary obtainable, also
    certain erotic manuals from Elephantis in Egypt' (Robert Graves trans.
    Suetonius, Tiberius 43).
44. *Aretine*: Aretino was famous as a 'wanton' (i.e. pornographic) poet. See
    Introduction pp. 15-16.
45. *glasses*: mirrors.
48. *succubae*: a succuba was a female demon capable of having sexual inter-
    course with sleeping men; also slang for prostitute.
    mists: means here the atmosphere, the air in his house.
55. *sublimed*: Sublimation was another of the alchemist's terms: the trans-
    mutation of a substance into another state, especially one of greater
    purity.
63. *subtly of the fart*: In 1607, Henry Ludlow, M.P., expressed disapproval
    of a message from the House of Lords in what the manuscript calls a

Whom I will entertain still for that subject.
The few that would give out themselves to be   65
Court and town stallions and each-where belie
Ladies who are known most innocent for them:
Those will I beg to make me eunuchs of,
And they shall fan me with ten estrich tails
A-piece, made in a plume, to gather wind.   70
We will be brave, Puff, now we ha' the medicine.
My meat shall all come in in Indian shells,
Dishes of agate, set in gold, and studded
With emeralds, sapphires, hyacinths and rubies.
The tongues of carps, dormice, and camels' heels   75
Boiled i' the spirit of Sol, and dissolved pearl
(Apicius's diet 'gainst the epilepsy).
And I will eat these broths with spoons of amber,
Headed with diamond and carbuncle.
My foot-boy shall eat pheasants, calvered salmons,   80
Knots, godwits, lampreys. I myself will have
The beards of barbels served instead of salads,
Oiled mushrooms, and the swelling unctuous paps
Of a fat pregnant sow, newly cut off,
Dressed with an exquisite and poignant sauce.   85
For which I'll say unto my cook 'There's gold:
Go forth and be a knight'.
FACE   Sir, I'll go look
A little how it heightens.
MAMMON   Do (*exit* FACE). My shirts
I'll have of taffeta-sarsenet, soft and light

'peculiar manner'. Jonson himself wrote of the incident, though not so
very subtly, in *Epigram* cxxxiii:

> And sure, it was th'intent
> Of the gross fart, let late in parliament,
> Had it been seconded, and not in fume
> Vanish'd away.

66. *belie ladies*: untruthfully boast of their conquests.
69. *estrich*: old form of ostrich ('estridge' another).
71. *brave*: 'We will cut a dash, live in fine style.'
74. *hyacinth*: jacinth, a reddish-orange variety of zircon.
77. *Apicius's diet*: There were three famous gluttons of this name. This one
    is probably Marcus Gabius Apicius (*c.* A.D. 30), who ate through a fortune
    of £800,000, till a mere tenth remained, whereupon he hanged himself.
80. *calvered salmons*: 'Calvering' took several forms: probably here cutting
    the salmon into thin slices while alive and then pickling.
81. *Knots*: a bird of the snipe family, breeding in the Arctic Circle.
    godwits: a marsh bird like a curlew. In *Epigram* ci. Jonson invites a friend
    to supper promising 'godwit if we can get' it.
    lampreys: eel-like boneless fish with a sucking mouth.
82. *barbel*: a fish of the carp tribe, a kind of fleshy beard hanging from its
    mouth.
89. *taffeta-sarsenet*: as made by the Saracens; a very fine soft silk material.

As cobwebs. And for all my other raiment,   90
It shall be such as might provoke the Persian,
Were he to teach the world riot anew.
My gloves of fishes' and bird-skins perfumed
With gums of paradise and eastern air—
SURLY   And do you think to have the Stone with this?   95
MAMMON   No, I do think t'have all this with the Stone.
SURLY   Why, I have heard he must be *homo frugi*,
A pious, holy and religious man,
One free from mortal sin, a very virgin.
MAMMON   That makes it, sir, he is so. But I buy it.   100
My venture brings it me. He, honest wretch,
A notable, superstitious, good soul,
Has worn his knees bare and his slippers bald
With prayer and fasting for it. And, sir, let him
Do it alone for me still. Here he comes.   105
Not a profane word afore him: 'tis poison.

Scene 3

Enter SUBTLE

MAMMON   Good morrow, father.
SUBTLE   Gentle son, good morrow,
And to your friend there. What is he with you?
MAMMON   An heretic that I did bring along
In hope, sir, to convert him.
SUBTLE   Son, I doubt
You are covetous that thus you meet your time   5
I' the just point; prevent your day at morning.
This argues something worthy of a fear
Of importune and carnal appetite.
Take heed you do not cause the blessing leave you
With your ungoverned haste. I should be sorry   10
To see my labours, now e'en at perfection,
Got by long watching and large patience,
Not prosper, where my love and zeal hath placed 'em.
Which (heaven I call to witness, with yourself,
To whom I have poured my thoughts) in all my ends   15
Have looked no way but unto public good,
To pious uses and dear charity,

---

97. *homo frugi*: a frugal, abstemious person. This was common belief,
    e.g. a Chinese writer of the third century says 'The alchemist must pre-
    viously fast for a hundred days and purify himself by perfume'.
6. *i' the just point*: at the exact point. i.e. 'There is something suspicious
    about such partiality.'
    prevent: anticipate. i.e. 'You are so keen, thus early in the morning, to
    bring the day to its outcome.'

Now grown a prodigy with men. Wherein
If you, my son, should now prevaricate,
And to your own particular lusts employ   20
So great and catholic a bliss, be sure
A curse will follow, yea, and overtake
Your subtle and most secret ways.

MAMMON   I know, sir.
You shall not need to fear me. I but come
To ha' you confute this gentleman.

SURLY   Who is   25
Indeed, sir, somewhat costive of belief
Toward your Stone: would not be gulled.

SUBTLE   Well, son,
All that I can convince him in is this:
The work is done. Bright Sol is in his robe.
We have a medicine of the triple soul,   30
The glorified spirit. Thanks be to heaven,
And make us worthy of it. (*calling to* FACE) Ulen Spiegel!

FACE (*within*)   Anon, sir.

SUBTLE (*calling*)   Look well to the register,
And let your heat still lessen by degrees
To the aludels.

FACE (*within*)   Yes, sir.

SUBTLE   Did you look   35
O' the bolt's-head yet?

FACE (*within*)   Which? On D, sir?

SUBTLE   Ay,
What's the complexion?

FACE (*within*)   Whitish.

SUBTLE   Infuse vinegar
To draw his volatile substance and his tincture.
And let the water in Glass E be filtered

18. *grown a prodigy*: 'The exercise of charity is now so rare that it has almost come to be marvelled at as a 'prodigy', an event out of the course of nature.'
19. *prevaricate*: deviate (from the straight and narrow path of righteousness).
21. *catholic*: universal.
30. *triple soul*: Three spirits were supposed to join the soul to the body: the 'vital spirit' in the heart, the 'spirit natural' in the liver, and 'spirit animal' in the brain. An essence of these was somehow to be present in the alchemist's brew.
32. *Ulen Spiegel*: Till Eulenspiegel, a German peasant of the 14th century about whose practical jokes legends grew over the next two hundred years. In England he was known as 'Howleglass', or 'Owl-glass' (a literal translation of Ulenspiegel). Subtle calls Face by this name partly to establish his own role of dignified authority over volatile servant, partly for the impressive exoticism of a foreign name.
33. *register*: a metal plate regulating the heat of the furnace.
35. *aludels*: pear-shaped pots of earthenware or glass, open at the ends so that a series could be fitted one into another.

E

And put into the gripe's egg. Lute him well, 40
And leave him closed *in balneo*.
FACE (*within*)   I will, sir.
SURLY What a brave language here is! Next to canting!
SUBTLE I have another work you never saw, son,
That three days since passed the philosopher's wheel
In the lent heat of Athanor, and's become 45
Sulphur o' Nature.
MAMMON   But 'tis for me?
SUBTLE   What need you?
You have enough in that is perfect.
MAMMON   Oh, but—
SUBTLE Why, this is covetise!
MAMMON   No, I assure you
I shall employ it all in pious uses,
Founding of colleges and grammar schools, 50
Marrying young virgins, building hospitals,
And now and then a church.

Re-enter FACE

SUBTLE (*to* FACE) How now?
FACE   Sir, please you,
Shall I not change the filter?
SUBTLE   Marry, yes.
And bring me the complexion of Glass B. (*exit* FACE)
MAMMON Ha' you another?
SUBTLE   Yes, son, were I assured 55
Your piety were firm, we would not want
The means to glorify it. But I hope the best.
I mean to tinct C in sand-heat tomorrow,
And give him imbibition.
MAMMON   Of white oil?
SUBTLE No, sir, of red. F is come over the helm too, 60

40. *gripe's egg*: a vessel shaped like an egg (gripe = griffin, supposed to produce large eggs like an ostrich).
    lute: to enclose it in clay as a protection against the heat.
41. *in balneo*: in a bath of hot water or sand so that the heating should be gradual.
42. *canting*: usually thieves' slang, also professional jargon of any kind, particularly the language of religious fanatics.
44. *philosopher's wheel*: the cycle of alchemical processes.
45. *lent heat of Athanor*: the slow fire of a special kind of furnace in which constant heat is maintained.
46. *sulphur o' nature*: red and white sulphur were supposed to be combined with pure mercury, contained by coal and silver.
47. *in that is perfect*: 'in that which is perfect'.
59. *imbibition*: soaking or saturating the substance with liquid, producing a combination of solid and liquid.

I thank my Maker, in Saint Mary's bath,
And shows *Lac Virginis*. Blessed be heaven!
I sent you of his faeces there, calcined.
Out of that calx I ha' won the salt of mercury.

MAMMON   By pouring on your rectified water?   65

SUBTLE   Yes, and reverberating in Athanor.

Re-enter FACE

How now? What colour says it?

FACE   The ground black, sir.

MAMMON   That's your crow's head?

SURLY   Your coxcomb's, is it not?

SUBTLE   No, 'tis not perfect. Would it were the crow.
That work wants something.

SURLY (*aside*)   Oh, I looked for this—   70
The hay is a-pitching.

SUBTLE   Are you sure you loosed 'em
I' their own menstrue?

FACE   Yes, sir and then married 'em,
And put 'em in a bolt's-head nipped to digestion
According as you bad me, when I set
The liquor of Mars to circulation   75
In the same heat.

SUBTLE   The process, then, was right.

FACE   Yes, by the token, sir, the retort brake,
And what was saved was put into the pelican

61. *Saint Mary's bath*: 'balneo Mariae' was another kind of sand or water bath.
62. *lac virginis*: 'white water', mercury.
63. *faeces*: sediment of the substance.
    calcined: burnt like lime and reduced to a calx, all its volatile parts being consumed.
64. *calx*: a powder produced by 'calcining'.
    salt of mercury: mercury oxide.
65. *rectified*: purified by renewed distillation.
66. *reverberating*: in a reverberating furnace the flame is forced back from the top upon the substance placed at the bottom.
68. *crow's head*: 'the black crow sometimes means lead' (Holmyard).
71. *the hay is a-pitching*: A hay was a net stretched across rabbit holes, into which the rabbits were then 'bolted' (see Surly's next aside l. 80). If the hay pitched, then it was insecure and the rabbit would escape. Surly means that he sees Subtle preparing a loop-hole for his own escape: Subtle is cunningly introducing the information that something has gone wrong, and will later exploit this to excuse his failure to produce the Stone.
73. *nipped to digestion*: the long neck of the flask was 'nipped' so that the soluble constituents of the substance heated in liquid may be extracted.
75. *liquor of Mars*: molten iron.
78. *pelican*: a special kind of still, having some resemblance in shape to the bird, and used for distilling and then redistilling the residue (probably hundreds of times over).

And signed with Hermes' seal.
SUBTLE   I think 'twas so.
We should have a new amalgama.
SURLY (aside)   Oh, this ferret   80
Is rank as any pole-cat.
SUBTLE   But I care not.
Let him e'en die. We have enough beside
In embrion. H has his white shirt on?
FACE   Yes, sir,
He's ripe for inceration. He stands warm
In his ash-fire. I would not you should let   85
Any die now, if I might counsel, sir,
For luck's sake to the rest. It is not good.
MAMMON He says right.
SURLY (aside)   Ay, are you bolted?
FACE   Nay, I know't, sir.
I have seen th'ill fortune. What is some three ounces
Of fresh materials?
MAMMON   Is't no more?
FACE   No more, sir,   90
Of gold, t' amalgam with some six of mercury.
MAMMON Away, here's money. What will serve?
FACE   Ask him, sir.
MAMMON How much?
SUBTLE   Give him nine pound—you may gi' him
                                           [ten.
SURLY Yes, twenty and be cozened, do!
MAMMON (gives FACE the money)   There 'tis.
SUBTLE This needs not, but that you will have it so   95
To see conclusions of all. For two
Of our inferior works are at fixation.
A third is in ascension. Go your ways.
Ha' you set the oil of Luna in kemia?
FACE Yes, sir.
SUBTLE   And the philosopher's vinegar?
FACE   Ay. (exit)   100

79. Hermes' seal: heating the neck of the vessel, then twisting and sealing it.
80. amalgama: mixture.
  this ferret: Surly's three asides are all playing on the same metaphor or
  proverb. The 'hay' or net for catching rabbits was placed for the rabbits
  to be 'bolted' into (see l. 71 above).; or ferrets would be used to drive
  them out. If Subtle is a ferret, it must be that Mammon and the other
  gulls are his rabbits. Anyway, Surly thinks he stinks ('is rank').
84. inceration: covering with wax, or bringing to the consistency of moist wax.
88. are you bolted?: 'They've got you in the net, have they?'
98. in ascension: being evaporated.
99. oil of luna: white elixir.
  in kemia: set it up for chemical analysis.
100. philosopher's vinegar: mercury.

SURLY   We shall have a salad.
MAMMON   When do you make projection?
SUBTLE   Son, be not hasty. I exalt our medicine
By hanging him *in balneo vaporoso*,
And giving him solution, then congeal him;
And then dissolve him, then again congeal him;   105
For look, how oft I iterate the work,
So many times I add unto his virtue.
As if at first one ounce convert a hundred,
After his second loose he'll turn a thousand,
His third solution ten, his fourth a hundred,   110
After his fifth a thousand thousand ounces
Of any imperfect metal into pure
Silver or gold, in all examinations
As good as any of the natural mine.
Get you your stuff here against afternoon,   115
Your brass, your pewter and your andirons.
MAMMON   Not those of iron?
SUBTLE   Yes, you may bring them too.
We'll change all metals.
SURLY   I believe you in that.
MAMMON   Then I may send my spits?
SUBTLE   Yes, and your racks.
SURLY   And dripping-pans and pot-hangers and hooks?   120
Shall he not?
SUBTLE   If he please.
SURLY   —To be an ass.
SUBTLE   How, sir?
MAMMON   This gentleman you must bear withal.
I told you he had no faith.
SURLY   And little hope, sir,
But much less charity should I gull myself.
SUBTLE   Why, what have you observed, sir, in our art   125
Seems so impossible?
SURLY   But your whole work, no more.
That you should hatch gold in a furnace, sir,
As they do eggs in Egypt!
SUBTLE   Sir, do you
Believe that eggs are hatched so?
SURLY   If I should?

101. *salad*: Sulphur was the oil, Mercury the vinegar, and these compounded
    with gold and salt were called a salad.
103. *in balneo vaporoso*: in a bath of steam.
106. *how oft I iterate*: 'how many times I repeat the process'.
128. *eggs in Egypt*: Herford and Simpson quote Pliny as translated in 1635
    by Philemon Holland: 'there be some eggs that will come to be birds with-
    out sitting of the hen, even by the work of nature only, as a man may see
    the experience in the dunghills of Egypt'.

SUBTLE   Why, I think that the greater miracle.   130
No egg but differs from a chicken more
Than metals in themselves.
SURLY   That cannot be.
The egg's ordained by nature to that end,
And is a chicken *in potentia*.
SUBTLE   The same we say of lead and other metals,   135
Which would be gold if they had time.
MAMMON   And that
Our art doth further.
SUBTLE   Ay, for 'twere absurd
To think that nature in the earth bred gold
Perfect i' the instant. Something went before.
There must be remote matter.
SURLY   Ay, what is that?   140
SUBTLE   Marry, we say—
MAMMON   Aye, now it heats. Stand, father!
Pound him to dust!
SUBTLE   It is, of the one part,
A humid exhalation which we call
Materia liquida or the unctuous water.
On th' other part, a certain crass and viscous   145
Portion of earth, both which, concorporate,
Do make the elementary matter of gold,
Which is not yet *propria materia*,
But common to all metals and all stones.
For where it is forsaken of that moisture
And hath more dryness, it becomes a stone.   150
Where it retains more of the humid fatness,
It turns to sulphur or to quicksilver
Who are the parents of all other metals.
Nor can this remote matter suddenly   155
Progress so from extreme unto extreme
As to grow gold and leap o'er all the means.
Nature doth first beget th'imperfect; then
Proceeds she to the perfect. Of that airy
And oily water, mercury is engendered,   160

140. *remote matter*: the original elements which will combine to form a
    substance such as gold.
141. *now it heats*: 'Now he's warming up,' 'getting into his stride'.
143. *exhalation*: a vapour.
144. *unctuous*: oily or greasy.
145. *crass and viscous*: coarse or thick; glutinous, part-solid, part-liquid.
146. *concorporate*: united into one substance.
147-176. Subtle's arguments are taken from *Disquisitiones Magicae* by
    Martin Delrio, sometimes following word for word (Latin texts given by
    Herford and Simpson. Vol. X).
148. *propria materia*: a substance, pure and unique in its nature.
157. *leap o'er all the means*: bypass all the intermediary stages.

Sulphur o' the fat and earthy part, the one
(Which is the last) supplying the place of male,
The other of the female, in all metals.
Some do believe hermaphrodeity,
That both do act and suffer. But these two   165
Make the rest ductile, malleable, extensive.
And even in gold they are, for we do find
Seeds of them by our fire and gold in them,
And can produce the species of each metal
More perfect thence than nature doth in earth.   170
Beside, who doth not see in daily practice
Art can beget bees, hornets, beetles, wasps,
Out of the carcasses and dung of creatures,
Yea, scorpions of an herb, being rightly placed.
And these are living creatures, far more perfect   175
And excellent than metals.
MAMMON   Well said, father!
Nay, if he take you in hand, sir, with an argument,
He'll bray you in a mortar.
SURLY   Pray you, sir, stay.
Rather than I'll be brayed, sir, I'll believe
That alchemy is a pretty kind of game,   180
Somewhat like tricks o' the cards, to cheat a man
With charming.
SUBTLE   Sir?
SURLY   What else are all your terms,
Whereon no one o' your writers 'grees with other?
Of your elixir, your *lac virginis*,
Your stone, your medicine, and your chrysosperm,   185
Your sal, your sulphur, and your mercury,
Your oil of height, your tree of life, your blood,
Your marchesite, your tutie, your magnesia,

162. *supplying the place of male*: 'The theory of the unity of the world
   permeated by a universal spirit had a corollary in the assumption that
   every object in the universe possessed some sort of life. Metals grew, as
   did minerals, and were even attributed sex. A fertilised seed of gold could
   develop into a nugget, the Smoky exhalation was masculine and the
   vapours are feminine, and mercury was a womb in which embryonic
   metals could be gestated' (Holmyard).
178. *bray you in a mortar*: crush you to powder. A mortar is a cup-like
   vessel in which food or chemicals are pounded or ground.
185. *chrysosperm*: literally seed of gold, an alchemist's term Jonson found in
   Delrio.
186. *sal*: salt, cf. *Canon Yeoman's Prologue*: 'Sal tartre, alkaly, and sal
   preparat' (257).
187. *oil of height*: quicksilver.
   tree of life: elixir vitae (the elixir which would renew life).
188. *tutie*: tutty, a crude oxide of zinc found adhering to flues of furnaces
   where brass has been melted.

Your toad, your crow, your dragon, and your panther,
Your sun, your moon, your firmament, your adrop,   190
Your lato, azoch, zernich, chibrit, heautarit,
And then your red man, and your white woman,
With all your broths, your menstrues, and materials
Of piss and egg-shells, women's terms, man's blood,
Hair o' the head, burnt clouts, chalk, merds and clay,   195
Powder of bones, scalings of iron, glass,
And worlds of other strange ingredients
Would burst a man to name?
SUBTLE   And all these, named,
Intending but one thing, which art our writers
Used to obscure their art.
MAMMON   Sir, so I told him: 200
Because the simple idiot should not learn it
And make it vulgar.
SUBTLE   Was not all the knowledge
Of the Egyptians writ in mystic symbols?
Speak not the Scriptures oft in parables?
Are not the choicest fables of the poets,   205
That were the fountains and first springs of wisdom,
Wrapped in perplexed allegories?
MAMMON   I urged that,
And cleared to him that Sisyphus was damned
To roll the ceaseless stone only because
He would have made ours common. (DOL *appears at the door*)
                                        [Who is this?   210
SUBTLE   God's precious! What do you mean? Go in, good lady,
Let me entreat you (DOL *retires*) (*calls* FACE) Where's this
                                                [varlet?

FACE (*re-appearing*)   Sir?
SUBTLE   You very knave! Do you use me thus?
FACE   Wherein, sir?
SUBTLE   Go in and see, you traitor. Go! (*exit* FACE)
MAMMON   Who is it, sir?

189. *your toad*, etc.,: See Introduction p. 5.
    dragon: stood for mercury.
190. *adrop*: the lead out of which mercury was to be extracted for making
    the Philosopher's Stone.
191. *lato*: 'latten', a mixed metal, probably of copper and zinc.
    azoch: quicksilver.
    zernich: orpiment, yellow arsenic.
    chibrit: sulphur.
    heautarit: another term for quicksilver.
192. *red man . . . white woman*: sulphur and mercury, thought of as male and
    female.
208. *Sisyphus*: punished for fraud and avarice. Mammon is comparably
    cursed, 'rolling the ceaseless stone of alchemy' (Partridge: *The Broken
    Compass*).

SUBTLE   Nothing, sir. Nothing.

MAMMON   What's the matter, good sir?   215
I have not seen you thus distempered. Who is't?

SUBTLE   All arts have still had, sir, their adversaries,
But ours the most ignorant. (FACE *returns*) What now?

FACE   'Twas not my fault, sir. She would speak with you.

SUBTLE   Would she, sir? Follow me. (*exit*)

MAMMON   Stay, Lungs.

FACE   I dare not, sir.   220

MAMMON   Stay, man. What is she?

FACE   A lord's sister, sir.

MAMMON   How? Pray thee, stay.

FACE   She's mad, sir, and sent hither—
He'll be mad too.

MAMMON   I warrant thee. Why sent hither?

FACE   Sir, to be cured.

SUBTLE (*calling him off-stage*)   Why, rascal!

FACE (*to* MAMMON)   Lo you. (*calling*) Here, sir.

Exit FACE

MAMMON   'Fore God, a Bradamante! A brave piece!   225

SURLY   Heart, this is a bawdy-house! I'll be burnt else.

MAMMON   Oh, by this light, no! Do not wrong him. He's
Too scrupulous that way. It is his vice.
No, he's a rare physician, do him right.
An excellent Paracelsian, and has done   230
Strange cures with mineral physic. He deals all
With spirits, he. He will not hear a word
Of Galen, or his tedious recipes.

Re-enter FACE

How now, Lungs?

FACE   Softly, sir, speak softly. I meant
To ha' told your worship all. This must not hear.   235

MAMMON   No, he will not be gulled. Leave him alone.

216. *distempered*: annoyed, put out of temper. Dol's appearance is quite
deliberate; but Subtle pretends to be put out at the sight of such a dis-
traction from their severely righteous purposes.

224. *Lo you*: 'There! You see', meaning: 'It's as I told you—he's furious.'

225. *Bradamante*: a warrior maiden in the Italian poems *Orlando Inamorato*
(by Boiardo) and *Orlando Furioso* (by Ariosto).

230. *Paracelsian*: a follower of Paracelsus (Theophrastus of Hohenheim
1493–1541). One of the most important men in the history of alchemy,
contemptuous of traditional forms and preparing for the genuine chemist.

233. *Galen*: Claudius Galenus (A.D. 130–201), the most famous of classical
physicians. Mammon means that Subtle is a thorough-going alchemist,
who will have nothing to do with traditional remedies prescribed by the
medical profession.

235. *This must not hear*: i.e. Surly.

FACE Y'are very right, sir. She is a most rare scholar,
And is gone mad with studying Broughton's works.
If you but name a word touching the Hebrew,
She falls into her fit, and will discourse   240
So learnedly of genealogies,
As you would run mad too to hear her, sir.

MAMMON How might one do t'have conference with her, Lungs?

FACE Oh, divers have run mad upon the conference.
I do not know, sir. I am sent in haste   245
To fetch a vial.

SURLY   Be not gulled, Sir Mammon.

MAMMON Wherein? Pray ye, be patient.

SURLY   Yes, as you are,
And trust confederate knaves and bawds and whores.

MAMMON You are too foul, believe it. Come here, Ulen.
One word.

FACE   I dare not, in good faith.

MAMMON   Stay, knave.   250

FACE He's extreme angry that you saw her, sir.

MAMMON (giving him money) Drink that. What is she when
she's out of her fit?

FACE Oh, the most affablest creature, sir! So merry!
So pleasant! She'll mount you up like quicksilver
Over the helm, and circulate like oil,   255
A very vegetal; discourse of state,
Of mathematics, bawdry, anything—

MAMMON Is she no way accessible? No means,
No trick, to give a man a taste of her—wit—
Or so?

SUBTLE (off-stage) Ulen!

FACE   I'll come to you again, sir. (exit) 260

MAMMON Surly, I did not think one o' your breeding
Would traduce personages of worth.

SURLY   Sir Epicure,
Your friend to use, yet still loth to be gulled.
I do not like your philosophical bawds.
Their Stone is lechery enough to pay for,   265
Without this bait.

MAMMON   Heart, you abuse yourself.
I know the lady and her friends and means,
The original of this disaster. Her brother
Has told me all.

SURLY   And yet you ne'er saw her

238. Broughton's works: see p. 118 l. 92 note.
256. Vegetal: as a noun the word usually meant simply 'vegetable' (as in 1.i.
   39). Herford and Simpson suggest it is used here in the sense of Latin
   'vegetus', 'active', 'healthy'.

Till now?

MAMMON   Oh yes, but I forgot. I have, believe it,   270
One o' the treacherous't memories, I do think,
Of all mankind.

SURLY   What call you her—brother?

MAMMON   My Lord—
He will not have his name known, now I think on't.

SURLY   A very treacherous memory!

MAMMON   O' my faith—

SURLY   Tut, if you ha' it not about you, pass it   275
Till we meet next.

MAMMON   Nay, by this hand, 'tis true.
He's one I honour and my noble friend,
And I respect his house.

SURLY   Heart! Can it be
That a grave sir, a rich, that has no need,
A wise sir, too, at other times, should thus   280
With his own oaths and arguments make hard means
To gull himself? An this be your elixir,
Your *lapis mineralis* and your lunary,
Give me your honest trick yet at primero
Or gleek, and take your *lutum sapientis*,   285
Your *menstruum simplex*. I'll have gold before you
And with less danger of the quicksilver
Or the hot sulphur.

Re-enter FACE

FACE (to SURLY)   Here's one from Captain Face, sir,
Desires you to meet him i' the Temple Church
Some half-hour hence and upon earnest business.   290
(*He whispers to* MAMMON) Sir, if you please to quit us now, and
                                        [come
Again within two hours, you shall have

272. *her—brother*: punctuation suggested by the folio, where a comma
makes the speaker pause so as to introduce an ironical, sceptical tone into
'brother'.
283. *lunary*: mercury.
284. *primero*: a popular card game. Four hands were dealt to each player,
each card having three times its normal value. Described as 'a new
game' about 1550.
285. *gleek*: another game, for three players, each trying for a set of three
court cards of the same rank.
lutum sapientis: a substance mentioned by Lully; its ingredients included
potter's earth, flour and white of egg.
286. *menstruum simplex*: a plain solvent.
287. *danger of the quicksilver*, etc.: used by doctors for the cure of venereal
disease.
289. *the Temple Church*: a meeting place for lawyers, business men, and
clients. Face is alluding to the round church when he says 'I ha' walked
the round till now' in III, iii, 2.

My master busy examining o'the works,
And I will steal you in unto the party,
That you may see her converse. (*to* SURLY) Sir, shall I say   295
You'll meet the Captain's worship?
SURLY (*aside*)   Sir, I will.
But by attorney and to a second purpose.
Now I am sure it is a bawdy-house.
I'll swear it, were the Marshal here to thank me.
The naming this commander doth confirm it.   300
Don Face! Why, he's the most authentic dealer
I' these commodities! The superintendent
To all the quainter traffickers in town.
He is their visitor, and does appoint
Who lies with whom, and at what hour, what price,   305
Which gown, and in what smock, what fall, what tire.
Him will I prove by a third person to find
The subtleties of this dark labyrinth.
Which, if I do discover, dear Sir Mammon,
You'll give your poor friend leave, though no philosopher,   310
To laugh. For you that are, 'tis thought, shall weep.
FACE   Sir, he does pray you'll not forget.
SURLY   I will not, sir.
Sir Epicure, I shall leave you?
MAMMON   I follow you straight.

Exit SURLY

FACE   But do so, good sir, to avoid suspicion.
This gentleman has a parlous head.
MAMMON   But wilt thou, Ulen,   315
Be constant to thy promise?
FACE   As my life, sir.
MAMMON   And wilt thou insinuate what I am, and praise me?
And say I am a noble fellow?
FACE   Oh, what else, sir?

294. *the party*: the person, i.e. Dol.
295. *converse*: meant both talking and sexual intercourse (cf. Surly's 'Now I am sure it is a bawdy house').
302. *these commodities*: i.e., prostitution and cheating.
303. *quainter traffickers*: quaint meant 'skilled', 'clever'; 'traffickers' means dealers in 'these commodities'.
304. *their visitor*: an authority who inspects religious or educational establishments: here the bawdy-houses.
306. *what fall*: the bands around the neck, falling flat on the gown, not protruding like a ruff.
     tire: attire.
311. *you that are*: 'you who (unlike myself) are considered to be a philosopher.'
315. *parlous*: dangerously shrewd.

And that you'll make her royal with the Stone,
An empress; and yourself king of Bantam.   320
MAMMON   Wilt thou do this?
FACE   Will I, sir?
MAMMON   Lungs, my Lungs!
I love thee.
FACE   Send your stuff, sir, that my master
May busy himself about projection.
MAMMON   Th' hast witched me, rogue.   (*gives him money*)
                                            [Take, go.
FACE   Your jack and all, sir.
MAMMON   Thou art a villain—I will send my jack   325
And the weights too. Slave, I could bite thine ear.
Away, thou dost not care for me.
FACE   Not I, sir?
MAMMON   Come, I was born to make thee, my good weasel,
Set thee on a bench and ha' thee twirl a chain
With the best lords vermin of 'em all.
FACE   Away, sir!   330
MAMMON   A count, nay, a count-palatine—
FACE   Good sir, go!
MAMMON   —shall not advance thee better, no nor faster.

Exit SIR MAMMON

Scene 4

Enter DOL *and* SUBTLE

SUBTLE   Has he bit? Has he bit?
FACE   And swallowed too, my Subtle.
I ha' given him line and now he plays, i' faith.
SUBTLE   And shall we twitch him?
FACE   Thorough both the gills.
A wench is a rare bait with which a man
No sooner's taken but he straight firks mad.   5
SUBTLE   Dol, my Lord Whats'hum's sister, you must now
Bear yourself *statelich*.
DOL   Oh, let me alone.

320. *king of Bantam*: in Java, wealthy and at that time powerful.
324. *jack*: a drinking pot, usually of leather, but presumably here of metal.
   Face is squeezing everything he can out of Mammon, ostensibly to go
   into the furnace for 'projection'.
329. *twirl a chain*: chain of office as worn by stewards of great households.
331. *count-palatine*: the Earl of Chester and Duke of Lancaster have this
   title.
6. *Lord Whats'hums' sister*: reminding her that this is her new role.
7. *statelich*: in aristocratic style (the folio has it in black letters as a foreign
   word, but it is much the same as Chaucer's 'estatlich' in the description
   of the Prioress as 'estatlich of manere').

I'll not forget my race, I warrant you.
I'll keep my distance, laugh and talk aloud,
Have all the tricks of a proud scurvy lady,   10
And be as rude as her woman.
FACE   Well said, Sanguine.
SUBTLE   But will he send his andirons?
FACE   His jack too,
And's iron shoeing-horn. I ha' spoke to him. Well,
I must not lose my wary gamester yonder.
SUBTLE   Oh, Monsieur Caution that will not be gulled?   15
FACE   Ay, if I can strike a fine hook into him now!
The Temple Church, there I have cast mine angle.
Well, pray for me. I'll about it.

                    A knocking is heard

SUBTLE   What, more gudgeons!
Dol, scout, scout! Stay, Face, you must go to the door.
Pray God it be my Anabaptist. Who is't, Dol?   20
DOL   I know him not. He looks like a gold-end man.
SUBTLE   Gods so! 'Tis he. He said he would send. What call
                                                    [you him?
The sanctified elder, that should deal
For Mammon's jack and andirons. Let him in!
Stay, help me off first with my gown (*exit* FACE). Away,   25
Madame, to your withdrawing chamber (*exit* DOL). Now,
In a new tune, new gesture, but old language.
This fellow is sent from one negotiates with me
About the Stone too, for the holy brethren
Of Amsterdam, the exiled saints, that hope   30
To raise their discipline by it. I must use him
In some strange fashion now, to make him admire me.

11. *sanguine*: full-blooded and amorous.
19. *scout*: 'Look out of the window, (scout around) to see who it is'.
20. *Anabaptist*: a sect founded in 1521, believing in adult baptism by
    immersion; its zealots were narrowly puritanical.
21. *gold-end man*: Herford and Simpson quote as one of the Cries of London:
    'Have ye any ends of gold or silver.' Perhaps the austere pinched appear-
    ance of the puritan suggests a parsimonious hoarder of such bits and pieces.
22. *'Tis he. He said.*: Wholesome has had dealings with Subtle and promised
    to send one of the brethren to do business.
31. *raise their discipline*: increase the power of their order or organisation.
    use him: Subtle means he will have to 'put on an act', treating Ananias in
    some eccentric way to impress him. Hence all the concentrated technical
    jargon directed at Face, the high-handed 'Where is my drudge?' and the
    disconcertingly sudden address to Ananias.

Scene 5

Re-enter FACE with ANANIAS

SUBTLE   Where is my drudge?
FACE   Sir?
SUBTLE   Take away the recipient,
And rectify your menstrue from the phlegma.
Then pour it o' the Sol in the cucurbite
And let 'em macerate together.
FACE   Yes, sir.
And save the ground?
SUBTLE   No. *Terra damnata*   5
Must not have entrance in the work. Who are you?
ANANIAS   A faithful brother, if it please you.
SUBTLE   What's that?
A Lullianist? A Ripley? *Filius artis*?
Can you sublime and dulcify? calcine?
Know you the sapor pontic, sapor stiptic?   10
Or what is homogene or heterogene?
ANANIAS   I understand no heathen language, truly.
SUBTLE   Heathen, you Knipper-Doling! Is *Ars sacra*,

1. *recipient*: vessel for receiving or holding a liquid.
2. *phlegma*: 'One of the five 'principles' of bodies, also called water; any watery inodorous tasteless substance obtained by distillation' (*O.E.D*).
3. *sol*: gold.
   cucurbite: gourd-shaped retort.
4. *macerate*: soften in a liquid.
5. *Terra damnata*: the sediment at the bottom of the retort, thought of as earthy, and therefore inferior substance.
8. *Lullianist*: Lullius, Lully, or Raymund Lull, a mystic philosopher of the 13th century. The alchemical works attributed to him are apocryphal.
   Ripley: George Ripley, a 15th-century alchemist from Ripley in Yorkshire, popularised the work attributed to Lully. His own writings were widely read. Subtle is indicating that the only kind of 'brethren' he is interested in are the alchemical sects.
   filius artis: son of the art (i.e. of alchemy).
9. *sublime*: turn a solid or liquid into a vapour.
   dulcify: wash the soluble salts out of a substance; neutralise the acidity.
   calcine: reduce to quick-lime (cf. p. 63. l. 63.)
10. *sapor pontic*: 'sapor' means savour, and was a term used by the alchemists to indicate the nature or condition of the substance under examination. Norton (1477) writes: 'So is the sowerish taste called Sapor Pontic, and less sour also called Sapor Stiptic'.
11. *homogene or heterogene*: old forms of homogeneous and heterogeneous.
13. *Knipper-Doling*: Bernt Knipperdollinck, a leader of the Anabaptist rising at Munster in 1534. The two years in which the 'Saints' established their kingdom were notorious for tyranny and debauchery. Subtle pretends to be scandalised by Ananias' ignorance, and then to 'place' him by alluding to this disreputable chapter in the Anabaptists' history.
    ars sacra: the sacred art of making the Philosopher's Stone.

Or chrysopoeia, or spagyrica,
Or the pamphysic, or panarchic knowledge   15
A heathen language?
ANANIAS   Heathen Greek, I take it.
SUBTLE   How? Heathen Greek?
ANANIAS   All's heathen but the Hebrew.
SUBTLE   Sirrah, my varlet, stand you forth and speak to
                                                   [him
Like a philosopher. Answer i'the language.
Name the vexations and the martyrizations   20
Of metals in the work.
FACE   Sir, putrefaction,
Solution, ablution, sublimation,
Cohobation, calcination, ceration, and
Fixation.
SUBTLE   This is heathen Greek to you now?
And when comes vivification?
FACE   . After mortification.   25
SUBTLE   What's cohobation?
FACE   'Tis the pouring on
Your *Aqua Regis* and then drawing him off
To the Trine Circle of the Seven Spheres.
SUBTLE   What's the proper passion of metals?
FACE   Malleation.
SUBTLE   What's your *Ultimum Supplicium Auri*?
FACE   Antimonium. 30
SUBTLE   This's heathen Greek to you? And what's your
                                          [Mercury?
FACE   A very fugitive: he will be gone, sir.
SUBTLE   How know you him?
FACE   By his viscosity,
His oleosity and his suscitability.

14. *chrysopoeia*: making gold.
    spagirica: the science of alchemy, a term probably invented by Paracelsus.
15. *pamphysic*: knowledge of all nature.
    panarchic: all-ruling.
25. *vivification*: restoration of a metal to its original state.
    mortification: alteration of the form of metals, etc. Destruction or neutral-
    ization of the active qualities of chemical substances (e.g. when mercury is
    dissolved in an acid menstruum).
27. *aqua regis*: or *aqua regia*, a mixture of nitric and hydrochloric acids
    which can dissolve the 'noble' metals, gold and platinum.
28. *Trine circle*: a circle divided into thirds, with three planets each 120°
    apart.
29. *malleation*: to malleate is to beat with a hammer.
30. *ultimum supplicium auri*: the literal meaning makes little sense ('the
    last punishment of gold').
    antimonium: native trisulphide.
34. *suscitability*: excitability.

SUBTLE   How do you sublime him?
FACE   With the calce of egg-shells,   35
White marble, talc.
SUBTLE   Your magisterium now?
What's that?
FACE   Shifting, sir, your elements,
Dry into cold, cold into moist, moist into hot,
Hot into dry.
SUBTLE   This's heathen Greek to you still?
Your *lapis philosophicus*?
FACE   'Tis a stone and not   40
A stone; a spirit, a soul, and a body,
Which, if you do dissolve, it is dissolved,
If you coagulate, it is coagulated,
If you make it to fly, it flieth.
SUBTLE   Enough. (*exit* FACE)
This's heathen Greek to you? What are you, sir?   45
ANANIAS   Please you, a servant of the exiled brethren,
That deal with widows' and with orphans' goods,
And make a just account unto the saints.
A deacon.
SUBTLE   Oh, you are sent from master Wholesome,
Your teacher?
ANANIAS   From Tribulation Wholesome,   50
Our very zealous pastor.
SUBTLE   Good. I have
Some orphans' goods to come here.
ANANIAS   Of what kind, sir?
SUBTLE   Pewter and brass, andirons and kitchen ware;
Metals that we must use our medicine on,
Wherein the brethren may have a penn'orth   55
For ready money.
ANANIAS   Were the orphans' parents
Sincere professors?
SUBTLE   Why do you ask?
ANANIAS   Because
We then are to deal justly, and give in truth
Their utmost value.
SUBTLE   'Slid, you'd cozen else
An if their parents were not of the faithful!   60

35. *calce of egg-shells*: the egg was symbolic. The hatching process en-
  couraged alchemists to believe that their schemes for hatching gold were
  part of nature (cf. Subtle's argument p. 66. ll. 130–2).
36. *magisterium*: magistery, the master-principle of nature, or (to the
  alchemist) the power of changing one substance into another.
49. *deacon*: an assistant to the Pastor in the anabaptist church.
54. *use our medicine on*: apply our art to change the metals to gold.
57. *professors*: i.e. of the faith.

  F

I will not trust you, now I think on't,
Till I ha' talked with your pastor. Ha' you brought money
To buy more coals?

ANANIAS   No, surely.

SUBTLE   No? How so?

ANANIAS   The brethren bid me say unto you, sir,
Surely they will not venture any more,   65
Till they may see projection.

SUBTLE   How?

ANANIAS   You have had
For the instruments, as bricks and loam and glasses,
Already thirty pound, and for materials,
They say, some ninety more. And they have heard, since,
That one at Heidelberg made it of an egg   70
And a small paper of pin-dust.

SUBTLE   What's your name?

ANANIAS   My name is Ananias.

SUBTLE   Out! The varlet
That cozened the Apostles! Hence, away,
Flee, Mischief! Had your holy consistory
No name to send me of another sound   75
Than wicked Ananias? Send your elders
Hither to make atonement for you quickly,
And gi' me satisfaction. Or out goes
The fire, and down th'alembics and the furnace,
Piger Henricus or what-not. Thou wretch!   80
Both Sericon and Bufo shall be lost,
Tell them. All hope of rooting out the bishops
Or the antichristian hierarchy shall perish
If they stay threescore minutes. The aqueity,
Terreity and sulphureity   85
Shall run together again, and all be annulled,
Thou wicked Ananias.

Exit ANANIAS

71. *pin-dust*: metal for making pins.
73. *cozened the Apostles*: Ananias and his wife Sapphira were among the
   first Christians. They stole from the community, were exposed by St
   Peter, and on being themselves denounced instantly expired (Acts. V, i–x).
74. *consistory*: council of church authorities.
79. *alembics*: the retorts used for distilling.
80. *piger Henricus*: 'a composite furnace constructed round a central com-
   partment and fed by one fire through apertures conducting the heat to the
   side furnaces, (Herford and Simpson); 'piger' = lazy, slothful (you didn't
   have to keep watching it).
81. *Sericon*: supposed to be an ingredient of 'the ferment of gold'. The red
   tincture.
   Bufo: the black tincture (literally 'a toad').
84. *aqueity*, etc.: These are the ingredients, of water, earth and fire, that are
   supposed to have made up the clarified mercury.

This will fetch 'em
And make 'em haste towards their gulling more.
A man must deal like a rough nurse and fright
Those that are froward to an appetite.   90

Scene 6

Enter FACE *and* DRUGGER

FACE (*to* DRUGGER)   He's busy with his spirits, but we'll upon
[him.
SUBTLE   How now? What mates? What Bayards ha' we here?
FACE   I told you he would be furious. Sir, here's Nab
Has brought you another piece of gold to look on
(We must appease him. Give it me), and prays you   5
You would devise—what is it, Nab?
DRUGGER   A sign, sir.
FACE   Ay, a good lucky one, a thriving sign, Doctor.
SUBTLE   I was devising now.
FACE (*aside to* SUBTLE)   'Slight, do not say so.
He will repent he ga' you any more.
(*aloud*) What say you to his constellation, Doctor?   10
The balance?
SUBTLE   No, that way is stale and common.
A townsman born in Taurus gives the bull
Or the bull's head; in Aries, the ram.
A poor device. No, I will have his name
Formed in some mystic character, whose radii   15
Striking the senses of the passers-by
Shall, by a virtual influence, breed affections
That may result upon the party owns it.
As thus—
FACE   Nab!
SUBTLE   He first shall have a *bell*. That's *Abel*
And by it, standing, one whose name is *Dee*,   20
In a *rug* gown. There's *D* and *Rug*, that's *Drug*.
And right against him, a dog snarling '*Er*'.
There's *Drugger*, Abel Drugger! That's his sign,

90. *froward*: difficult to manage, 'naughty' as the nurse might say of a child.
2. *mates*: contemptuously used (cf. *Taming of the Shrew*, I, i, 58).
   Bayards: wild horses (Bayard was the name of a magic horse, and 'as bold
   as Blind Bayard' became a proverbial saying applying to ungovernable,
   headstrong folk).
11. *The balance*: the sign of Libra.
19. *Nab!*: a nudging aside to Drugger, with the sense of 'Look what he's
   going to do for you . . . Aren't you excited?'
20. *Dee*: John Dee, mathematician, astrologer and quack, died two years
   before *The Alchemist* was written. (See Introduction, p. 6).
21. *rug*: made of a hairy frieze and commonly worn by astrologers.

And here's now mystery and hieroglyphic!

FACE Abel, thou art made.

DRUGGER   Sir, I do thank his worship.   25

FACE Six o'thy legs more will not do it, Nab.
He has brought you a pipe of tobacco, Doctor.

DRUGGER   Yes, sir.
I have another thing I would impart—

FACE Out with it, Nab.

DRUGGER   Sir, there is lodged, hard by me,
A rich young widow—

FACE   Good! A bona roba?   30

DRUGGER But nineteen at the most.

FACE   Very good, Abel.

DRUGGER Marry, she's not in fashion yet. She wears
A hood, but 't stands a-cop.

FACE   No matter, Abel.

DRUGGER And I do, now and then, give her a fucus—

FACE What! Dost thou deal, Nab?

SUBTLE   I did tell you, Captain.   35

DRUGGER And physic too sometime, sir, for which she trusts me
With all her mind. She's come up here of purpose
To learn the fashion.

FACE   Good (his match too!). On, Nab.

DRUGGER And she does strangely long to know her fortune.

FACE God's lid, Nab! Send her to the Doctor hither.   40

DRUGGER Yes, I have spoken to her of his worship already,
But she's afraid it will be blown abroad,
And hurt her marriage.

FACE   Hurt it? 'Tis the way
To heal it if 'twere hurt, to make it more
Followed and sought. Nab, thou shalt tell her this.   45
She'll be more known, more talked of, and your widows
Are ne'er of any price till they be famous:
Their honour is their multitude of suitors.
Send her. It may be thy good fortune. What?
Thou dost not know.

DRUGGER   No, sir, she'll never marry   50
Under a knight. Her brother has made a vow.

24. *mystery*: sign of his trade (or mystery).
   hieroglyphic: a sign with hidden, symbolic meaning.
26. *six o' thy legs more*: Drugger has bowed his respects and gratitude. Face
   means 'Mere bowing won't suffice, however often repeated': i.e. he must
   show some more solid token of appreciation.
30. *bona roba*: a courtesan (cf. Henry IV Pt. 2, III, ii, 24–5).
33. *a-cop*: over the back of the head.
34. *fucus*: cosmetics and probably love-philtres also.
35. *deal*: Face takes up the sense of the sale of love-philters: 'deal' in
   Elizabethan slang meant involvement in prostitution.

FACE   What, and dost thou despair, my little Nab,
   Knowing what the Doctor has set down for thee,
   And seeing so many o' the city dubbed?
   One glass o' thy water with a madame I know   55
   Will have it done, Nab. What's her brother? A knight?
DRUGGER   No, sir: a gentleman, newly warm in his land, sir,
   Scarce cold in his one and twenty, that does govern
   His sister here, and is a man himself
   Of some three thousand a year, and is come up   60
   To learn to quarrel and to live by his wits,
   And will go down again and die i' the country.
FACE   How! to quarrel?
DRUGGER   Yes, sir, to carry quarrels
   As gallants do, and manage 'em by line.
FACE   'Slid, Nab! The Doctor is the only man   65
   In Christendom for him! He has made a table
   With mathematical demonstrations
   Touching the art of quarrels. He will give him
   An instrument to quarrel by. Go, bring 'em both:
   Him and his sister. And, for thee, with her   70
   The Doctor happily may persuade. Go to.
   Shalt give his worship a new damask suit
   Upon the premises.
SUBTLE   Oh, good Captain!
FACE   He shall.
   He is the honestest fellow, Doctor. Stay not.
   No offers! Bring the damask, and the parties.   75
DRUGGER   I'll try my power, sir.
FACE   And thy will, too, Nab.
SUBTLE   'Tis good tobacco, this! What is't an ounce?
FACE   He'll send you a pound, Doctor.
SUBTLE   Oh no!
FACE   He will do't.
   It is the goodest soul. Abel, about it!
   (*aside to* DRUGGER) Thou shalt know more anon. Away, be gone.   80

Exit DRUGGER

   A miserable rogue, and lives with cheese,
   And has the worms. That was the cause indeed
   Why he came now. He dealt with me, in private,
   To get a medicine for 'em.
SUBTLE   And shall, sir. This works!
FACE   A wife! A wife for one on's, my dear Subtle.   85

---

54. *dubbed*: knighted. James I's generosity in dispensing knighthoods had
   become a joke.
64. *by line*: according to the rules (see p. 94. l. 26 note, and p. 95 ll. 38 and 39).

We'll e'en draw lots, and he that fails shall have
The more in goods the other has in tail.

SUBTLE   Rather the less, for she may be so light
She may want grains.

FACE   Ay, or be such a burden
A man would scarce endure her for the whole.   90

SUBTLE   Faith, best let's see her first, and then determine.

FACE   Content. But Dol must ha' no breath on't.

SUBTLE   Mum.
Away you to your Surly yonder. Catch him.

FACE   Pray God I ha' not stayed too long!

SUBTLE   I fear it.

Exeunt

87. *in tail*: legal term for possession of an estate on condition that it reverts
to the donor on the death of the possessor or the failure of his line. Also
slang for the private parts.
88. *light*: loose morals.
89. *grains*: to make up weight (involving a pun on 'light').

ACT III

Scene 1: The lane before Lovewit's house

Enter TRIBULATION WHOLESOME *and* ANANIAS

TRIBULATION   These chastisements are common to the saints,
And such rebukes we of the Separation
Must bear with willing shoulders as the trials
Sent forth to tempt our frailties.

ANANIAS   In pure zeal,
I do not like the man. He is a heathen,   5
And speaks the language of Canaan, truly.

TRIBULATION   I think him a profane person indeed.

ANANIAS   He bears
The visible mark of the Beast in his forehead.
And for his Stone, it is a work of darkness,
And with philosophy blinds the eyes of man.   10

TRIBULATION   Good brother, we must bend unto all means
That may give furtherance to the holy cause.

ANANIAS   Which his cannot. The sanctified cause
Should have a sanctified course.

TRIBULATION   Not always necessary.
The children of perdition are oft-times   15
Made instruments even of the greatest works.
Beside, we should give somewhat to man's nature,
The place he lives in, still about the fire
And fume of metals that intoxicate
The brain of man and make him prone to passion.   20
Where have you greater atheists than your cooks?
Or more profane or choleric than your glass-men?
More antichristian than your bell-founders?
What makes the devil so devilish, I would ask you,
Satan, our common enemy, but his being   25

4. *In pure zeal*: i.e. speaking out of the purest motives of religious enthusiasm, nothing personal about it. 'Zeal' a cant word, always picked on by writers satirising the Puritan sects.
6. *language of Canaan*: a heathen tongue.
8. *mark of the Beast*: Revelation xix. 20. 'And the beast was taken, and with him the false prophet that wrought miracles before him, with which he deceived them that had received the mark of the beast, and them that worshipped his image.' Also xvi. 2.
21. *greater atheists than your cooks*: Herford and Simpson quote from Earle's *Microcosmographie* (1628) no. 42. '*A Cook*: the kitchen is his hell, and he the devil in it, where his meat and he fry together. . . . He is never good Christian till a hissing pot of ale has slaked him, like water cast on a fire-brand, and for that time he is tame and dispossessed.'
23. *bell-founders*: bell-makers.

83

Perpetually about the fire, and boiling
Brimstone and arsenic. We must give, I say,
Unto the motives and the stirrers-up
Of humours in the blood. It may be so,
When as the work is done, the Stone is made,   30
This heat of his may turn into a zeal,
And stand up for the beauteous discipline
Against the menstruous cloth and rag of Rome.
We must await his calling and the coming
Of the good spirit. You did fault t'upbraid him   35
With the brethren's blessing of Heidelberg, weighing
What need we have to hasten on the work
For the restoring of the silenced saints,
Which ne'er will be, but by the Philosopher's Stone.
And so a learned elder, one of Scotland,   40
Assured me, *aurum potabile* being
The only medicine for the civil magistrate
T'incline him to a feeling of the cause,
And must be daily used in the disease.

ANANIAS   I have not edified more, truly, by man,   45
Not since the beautiful light first shone on me,
And I am sad my zeal hath so offended.

TRIBULATION   Let us call on him, then.

ANANIAS   The motion's good,
And of the spirit. I will knock first. (*knocks and
calls*) Peace be within! (*a door is opened and they enter*)

Scene 2

A room in Lovewit's house

Enter SUBTLE, *followed by* TRIBULATION *and* ANANIAS

SUBTLE   Oh, are you come? 'Twas time. Your threescore minutes
Were at the last thread, you see; and down had gone
Furnus acediae, turris circulatorius;

28. *motives*: the forces that move, or stimulate the 'humours' (that is, the
    dominant personal characteristics).
36. *Heidelberg*: a strongly Protestant university. The Heidelberg Catechism,
    a famous document of the Reformation, carried the authority of all the
    foremost Lutherans. Ananias has used some of their pronouncements as
    weapons against Subtle.
38. *silenced saints*: the fifty to three-hundred clergy who left the Church
    after the Convocation of 1604 had passed laws excommunicating non-
    conformists.
41. *aurum potabile*: drinkable gold: 'a preparation of nitro-muriate of gold
    deoxydized by some volatile oil, formerly esteemed as a cordial medicine'
    (*O.E.D.*).
3. *Furnus acediae*: another name for the *piger Henricus* furnace (p. 78, l. 80
   note); *acedia* = sloth (medieval latin).
   turris circulatorius: the furnaces for alchemy were generally shaped like
   small round towers.

Lambec, bolt's-head, retort and pelican
Had all been cinders. Wicked Ananias!   5
Art thou returned? Nay, then, it goes down yet.
TRIBULATION   Sir, be appeased. He is come to humble
Himself in spirit and to ask your patience
If too much zeal hath carried him aside
From the due path.
SUBTLE   Why, this doth qualify!   10
TRIBULATION   The brethren had no purpose, verily,
To give you the least grievance, but are ready
To lend their willing hands to any project
The spirit and you direct.
SUBTLE   This qualifies more!
TRIBULATION   And for the orphans' goods, let them be valued; 15
Or what is needful else to the holy work,
It shall be numbered. Here by me, the saints
Throw down their purse before you.
SUBTLE   This qualifies most!
Why, thus it should be; now you understand!
Have I discoursed so unto you of our Stone   20
And of the good that it shall bring your cause,
Showed you, beside, the main of hiring forces
Abroad, drawing the Hollanders, your friends,
From the Indies to serve you with all their fleet,
That even the medicinal use shall make you a faction   25
And party in the realm? As put the case
That some great man in state, he have the gout,
Why, you but send three drops of your clixir,
You help him straight: there you have made a friend.
Another has the palsy, or the dropsy: 30
He takes of your incombustible stuff,
He's young again: there you have made a friend.
A lady, that is past the feat of body,
Though not of mind, and hath her face decayed
Beyond all cure of paintings, you restore   35
With the oil of talc: there you have made a friend:
And all her friends. A lord that is a leper,
A knight that has the bone-ache, or a squire
That hath both these, you make 'em smooth and sound

4. *lambec*: alembic for distillation. For the other terms see notes on p. 56
   (bolt's head), p. 63 (pelican).
31. *incombustible stuff*: an oil, a sort of elixir, supposed to be produced
   through the power of the Philosopher's Stone.
35. *paintings*: cosmetics.
36. *oil of talc*: a cheap cosmetic made in England used for whitening the
   complexion.
38. *the bone-ache*: syphilis. cf. *Troilus and Cressida* (II, iii, 18).

With a bare fricace of your medicine: still   40
You increase your friends.

TRIBULATION   Ay, 'tis very pregnant.

SUBTLE   And then the turning of this lawyer's pewter
To plate at Christmas—

ANANIAS   Christ-tide, I pray you.

SUBTLE   Yet, Ananias?

ANANIAS   I have done.

SUBTLE   Or changing
His parcel gilt to massy gold. You cannot   45
But raise you friends: withal, to be of power
To pay an army in the field, to buy
The king of France out of his realms, or Spain
Out of his Indies. What can you not do
Against lords spiritual or temporal   50
That shall oppone you?

TRIBULATION   Verily, 'tis true.
We may be temporal lords ourselves, I take it.

SUBTLE   You may be anything, and leave off to make
Long-winded exercises, or suck up
Your ha and hum in tune. I not deny   55
But such as are not graced in a state
May, for their cnds, be adverse in religion,
And get a tune to call the flock together.
For, to say sooth, a tune does much with women
And other phlegmatic people; it is your bell.   60

ANANIAS   Bells are profane; a tune may be religious.

SUBTLE   No warning with you? Then farewell my patience.
'Slight, it shall down! I will not be thus tortured.

TRIBULATION   I pray you, sir.

SUBTLE   All shall perish! I have spoke it.

TRIBULATION   Let me find grace, sir, in your eyes. The man   65
He stands corrected. Neither did his zeal
(But as yourself) allow a tune somewhere,

---

40. *fricace*: rubbing.
43. *Christ-tide*: the 'mass' in 'Christmas' is intolerably Popish in Ananias'
ears. The puritans changed any such words (Lammas, Michaelmas,
Candlemas) so that the offensive syllable was removed and 'tide' substi-
tuted.
45. *parcel gilt*: a piece of silver partly gilded.
51. *oppone*: oppose.
55. *ha and hum*: exclamations thought typical of the Puritan preacher.
Subtle is living up to his name here, for his implications are that Tribulation and his brethren are hypocrites who need to put on an act of gravity
and devotion, tedious to them as well as to everyone else, and one from
which possession of the Stone would release them.
66. *neither did his zeal*: Ananias (says Wholesome) permitted 'a tune' only
as an expedient (as did Subtle), and this, with the Stone in possession, will
no longer be necessary.

Which now, being toward the Stone, we shall not need.
SUBTLE   No, nor your holy vizard to win widows
To give you legacies, or make zealous wives   70
To rob their husbands for the common cause,
Nor take the start of bonds broke but one day
And say they were forfeited by providence.
Nor shall you need o'er night to eat huge meals
To celebrate your next day's fast the better,   75
The whilst the brethren and the sisters, humbled,
Abate the stiffness of the flesh. Nor cast
Before your hungry hearers scrupulous bones,
As whether a Christian may hawk or hunt,
Or whether matrons of the holy assembly   80
May lay their hair out or wear doublets,
Or have that idol starch about their linen.
ANANIAS   It is indeed an idol.
TRIBULATION   Mind him not, sir.
(to ANANIAS) I do command thee, spirit of zeal but trouble,
To peace within him. Pray you, sir, go on.   85
SUBTLE   Nor shall you need to libel 'gainst the prelates
And shorten so your ears against the hearing
Of the next wire-drawn grace. Nor of necessity
Rail against plays to please the alderman
Whose daily custard you devour. Nor lie   90
With zealous rage till you are hoarse. Not one

70. *zealous wives*: i.e. puritan wives.
72. *bonds broke*: taking the opportunity to exact a fine for the most trifling
   infringements.
77. *stiffness of the flesh*: The flesh, or the appetite for things of this world, is
   unyielding, loath to be subject to the moral dictates of the spirit.
78–82. *scrupulous bones* etc.: points of argument involving high principles
   concerning behaviour. Hawking and hunting were sports that might
   well go with riotous living; care of the hair was a vanity; starch, used
   for stiffening ruffs, was known by puritans as 'the devil's liquor'; and
   for women to wear doublets was to transgress the law as laid down in
   Deuteronomy xxii.
84–85. *(to Ananias)*: words intended to keep Ananias quiet, but nominally
   addressed to the 'spirit' inside him. He intimates that Ananias is possessed
   by a spirit, and an equivocal one, because although full of righteousness it
   is also a great nuisance.
86–87. *libel 'gainst the prelates*: the campaign of the puritans against the
   bishops, whom they regarded as little better than papists, was already
   fierce. Herford and Simpson quote the case of Alexander Leighton whose
   tract against the bishops (1628) brought him before the Star Chamber where
   he was condemned to be fined, pilloried, flogged and de-eared (hence the
   pun in 'shorten your ears').
88. *wire-drawn grace*: drawn-out, cf. 'a dry grace, as long as thy tablecloth'
   (*Bartholomew Fair*, I, iii, 87).
89. *rail against plays . . .*: the puritans regarded the theatre as Satan's special
   playground. The city authorities were their allies; complaints from the
   middle classes against theatres as centres of disorder commonly came
   before the Queen, who would then generally defend the players.

Of these so singular arts. Nor call yourselves
By names of Tribulation, Persecution,
Restraint, Long-Patience, and such like, affected
By the whole family, or wood of you   95
Only for glory and to catch the ear
Of the disciple.
TRIBULATION Truly sir, they are
Ways that the godly brethren have invented
For propagation of the glorious cause,
As very notable means, and whereby also   100
Themselves grow soon and profitably famous.
SUBTLE Oh, but the Stone! All's idle to it! Nothing!
The art of angels, nature's miracle,
The divine secret that doth fly in clouds
From east to west and whose tradition   105
Is not from men but spirits.
ANANIAS   I hate traditions.
I do not trust them—
TRIBULATION   Peace!
ANANIAS   They are popish all.
I will not peace. I will not—
TRIBULATION   Ananias!
ANANIAS Please the profane to grieve the godly, I may not.
SUBTLE Well, Ananias, thou shalt overcome.   110
TRIBULATION It is an ignorant zeal that haunts him, sir,
But truly else a very faithful brother;
A botcher, and a man by revelation
That hath a competent knowledge of the truth.
SUBTLE Has he a competent sum there i' the bag   115
To buy the goods within? I am made guardian,
And must, for charity and conscience sake,
Now see the most be made for my poor orphan,
Though I desire the brethren, too, good gainers.
There they are, within. When you have viewed and bought 'em,   120
And ta'en the inventory of what they are,
They are ready for projection. There's no more
To do. Cast on the medicine, so much silver
As there is tin there, so much gold as brass,
I'll gi' it you in, by weight.
TRIBULATION   But how long time,   125
Sir, must the saints expect yet?
SUBTLE   Let me see,

95. *wood*: 'the whole lot of you' (a collection or crowd).
113. *a botcher*: applied to puritans, but literally meaning a tailor who did
repairs. He would not make much money, and Wholesome's implication
is that Ananias is a poor, hard-working enthusiast for whom one should be
prepared to make allowances.
126. *expect*: wait (Latin 'expectare').

How's the moon, now? Eight, nine, ten days hence
He will be silver potate; then three days
Before he citronise. Some fifteen days
The Magisterium will be perfected.   130
ANANIAS About the second day of the third week
In the ninth month?
SUBTLE   Yes, my good Ananias.
TRIBULATION What will the orphans' good arise to, think you?
SUBTLE Some hundred marks, as much as filled three cars
Unladed now; you'll make six millions of 'em.   135
But I must ha' more coals laid in.
TRIBULATION   How?
SUBTLE   Another load,
And then we ha' finished. We must now increase
Our fire to *ignis ardens*. We are past
Fimus equinus, Balnei, Cineris,
And all those lenter heats. If the holy purse   140
Should with this draught fall low, and that the saints
Do need a present sum, I have a trick
To melt the pewter you shall buy now instantly,
And with a tincture make you as good Dutch dollars
As any are in Holland.
TRIBULATION   Can you so?   145
SUBTLE Ay, and shall bide the third examination.
ANANIAS It will be joyful tidings to the brethren.
SUBTLE But you must carry it secret.
TRIBULATION Ay, but stay:
This act of coining, is it lawful?
ANANIAS   Lawful?
We know no magistrate. Or, if we did,   150

128. *silver potate*: liquid silver (literally 'drunk' or 'drinking').
129. *citronise*: turn yellow, one of the stages in the process culminating in projection (cf. the poem quoted in the Introduction p. 5).
130. *Magisterium*: the power of changing one substance into another (cf. p. 77, l. 36, note).
134. *hundred marks*: £66 13s. 4d.
138. *ignis ardens*: burning fire.
139. *Fimus equinus*.: the 'equi clibanum', or 'heat of horse-dung' of p. 34, l. 83.
balnei: see p. 34, l. 41.
cineris: see p. 64, l. 84.
144. *good Dutch dollars*: Herford and Simpson quote the case of John Beish, a metal worker, who in 1599 was examined on his dealings with an alchemist called Scory of Petticoat Lane. This man had a scheme for counterfeiting coins ('dollars' in this case, as in the play), and then circulating them with the help of a merchant in Turkey, as Tribulation Wholesome and his brethren are hoping to do with the 'Dutch dollars' to which Subtle will help them.
150. *no magistrate*: the anabaptists held that as 'Christ is the King and Law-giver of the Church and conscience', no magistrate could have authority to 'meddle in religion or matters of conscience'.

This is foreign coin.
SUBTLE   It is no coining, sir.
It is but casting.
TRIBULATION   Ha? You distinguish well.
Casting of money may be lawful.
ANANIAS   'Tis, sir.
TRIBULATION   Truly, I take it so.
SUBTLE   There is no scruple,
Sir, to be made of it. Believe Ananias.   155
This case of conscience he is studied in.
TRIBULATION   I'll make a question of it to the brethren.
ANANIAS   The brethren shall approve it lawful, doubt not.
Where shall't be done?
SUBTLE   For that we'll talk anon. (*knocking off-*
                                                        [*stage*)
There's some to speak with me. Go in, I pray you,   160
And view the parcels. That's the inventory.
I'll come to you straight.

                    Exeunt TRIBULATION *and* ANANIAS

                        Who is it? Face! Appear.

                              SCENE 3

                      Enter FACE *in his uniform*

SUBTLE   How now? Good prize?
FACE   Good pox! Yond' costive
                                                        [cheater
Never came on.
SUBTLE   How then?
FACE   I ha' walked the round.
Till now, and no such thing.
SUBTLE   And ha' you quit him?
FACE   Quit him? An hell would quit him too, he were happy!
'Slight, would you have me stalk like a mill-jade   5
All day for one that will not yield us grains?
I know him of old.
SUBTLE   Oh, but to ha' gulled him

152. *but casting*: 'coining' means making counterfeit coins; 'casting' still
    means making coins but is less heavy with criminal associations.
  1. *costive*: literally, constipated. Perhaps a general term of abuse here,
    perhaps a way of characterising Surly's mean-spirited scepticism (cf.
    'costive of belief' p. 61, l. 26).
  2. *walked the round*: Face and Surly were to have met in the round Temple
    Church (see p. 71, l. 289, note).
  3. *quit him*: given him up.
  6. *grains*: money (cf. p. 82, l. 89).

Had been a maistry.

FACE   Let him go, black boy,
And turn thee that some fresh news may possess thee.
A noble count, a Don of Spain, my dear   10
Delicious compeer and my party-bawd,
Who is come hither, private, for his conscience,
And brought munition with him, six great slops,
Bigger than three Dutch hoys, beside round trunks
Furnished with pistolets and pieces of eight,   15
Will straight be here, my rogue, to have thy bath
(That is the colour) and to make his battery
Upon our Dol, our castle, our Cinque-Port,
Our Dover pier, our what thou wilt. Where is she?
She must prepare perfumes, delicate linen,   20
The bath in chief, a banquet, and her wit,
For she must milk his epididymis.
Where is the doxy?

SUBTLE   I'll send her to thee,
And but dispatch my brace of little John Leydens,
And come again myself.

FACE   Are they within, then?   25

SUBTLE   Numbering the sum.

FACE   How much?

SUBTLE   A hundred marks,
                                    [boy. (exit)

FACE   Why, this is a lucky day! Ten pounds of Mammon!
Three of my clerk! A portugue o' my grocer!
This o'the brethren? Besides reversions
And states to come, i' the widow and my count!   30
My share today will not be bought for forty—

Enter DOL

8. *a maistry*: stroke of genius.
13. *munition*: armaments. The military metaphor is continued in the
  following lines: 'to make his battery upon our Dol' etc.
  slops: wide baggy breeches worn at this time.
14. *Dutch hoys*: boats carrying passengers a short distance round the sea-
  coast.
15. *pistolets*: gold coin at this time worth about 16/6.
  pieces of eight: Spanish dollars worth about 4/6.
17. *that is the colour*: 'that is the excuse, the pretext on which I have persuaded him to come to you'.
22. *epididymis*: 'A long narrow structure attached to the posterior border of
  the adjoining outer surface of the testicle, and consisting chiefly of coils of
  the efferent duct, which emerge from it as the vas deferens' (*O.E.D.*).
23. *doxy*: slang term for a tramp's mistress.
24. *John Leydens*: i.e. the anabaptists. John of Leyden was their 'prophet',
  and established 'the kingdom of God', stamped out in 1536 (cf. p. 75, l. 13,
  note).
27. *mammon*: riches, money.
28. *portugue*: varied between £3 5s. to £4 10s. in value.

DOL   What?

FACE   Pounds, dainty Dorothy. Art thou so near?

DOL   Yes, say, Lord General, how fares our camp?

FACE   As with the few that had entrenched themselves
Safe by their discipline against a world, Dol,   35
And laughed within those trenches and grew fat
With thinking on the booties, Dol, brought in
Daily by their small parties. This dear hour
A doughty Don is taken, with my Dol;
And thou mayest make his ransom what thou wilt,   40
My Dousabell. He shall be brought here, fettered
With thy fair looks before he sees thee, and thrown
In a down-bed as dark as any dungeon,
Where thou shalt keep him waking with thy drum—
Thy drum, my Dol, thy drum—till he be tame   45
As the poor black-birds were i' the great frost,
Or bees are with a basin, and so hive him
I' the swan-skin coverlid and cambric sheets
Till he work honey and wax, my little God's gift.

DOL   What is he, General?

FACE   An Adalantado,   50
A Grandee, girl. Was not my Dapper here yet?

DOL   No.

FACE   Nor my Drugger?

DOL   Neither.

FACE   A pox on 'em.
They are so long a-furnishing! Such stinkards
Would not be seen upon these festival days.

Re-enter SUBTLE

How now? Ha' you done?

SUBTLE   Done. They are gone. The sum   55
Is here in bank, my Face. I would we knew
Another chapman, now, would buy 'em outright.

FACE   'Slid, Nab shall do't, against he ha' the widow
To furnish household.

---

33. *say, Lord General, how fares our camp?*: the opening line (after the In-
    duction) of Kyd's *Spanish Tragedy*, a popular play and a favourite quarry
    for mock-heroic remarks in conversation.
46. *the great frost*: the winter of 1607 to 1608 when the Thames was frozen
    over for three months.
48. *cambric*: a fine white linen originally made at Cambray in Flanders.
50. *Adalantado*: a grandee or governor of a province.
57. *chapman*: a merchant, dealer in buying and selling.
58. *against he ha' the widow*: Drugger, they think, will buy the stuff to help
    him set up house in preparation for the marriage he will hope to make
    with the rich widow.

SUBTLE   Excellent. Well thought on.
Pray God he come.
FACE   I pray he keep away   60
Till our new business be o'er-past.
SUBTLE   But, Face,
How cam'st thou by this secret Don?
FACE   A spirit
Brought me th'intelligence in a paper here
As I was conjuring yonder in my circle
For Surly. I ha' my flies abroad. Your bath   65
Is famous, Subtle, by my means. Sweet Dol,
You must go tune your virginal; no losing
O' the least time. And, do you hear? Good action.
Firk like a flounder, kiss like a scallop, close,
And tickle him with thy mother-tongue. His great 70
Verdugo-ship has not a jot of language.
So much the easier to be cozened, my Dolly.
He will come here in a hired coach, obscure,
And our own coach-man, whom I have sent as guide,
No creature else. (*knocking off-stage*) Who's that?
SUBTLE   It is not he?   75
FACE   Oh no, not yet this hour.
SUBTLE   Who is't?
DOL   Dapper,
Your clerk.
FACE   God's will then, Queen of Fairy,
On with your tire; and, Doctor, with your robes.
Let's dispatch him, for God's sake.   (*exit* DOL)
SUBTLE   'Twill be long.
FACE   I warrant you. Take but the cues I give you,   80
It shall be brief enough. 'Slight, here are more!
Abel, and I think the angry boy, the heir,
That fain would quarrel.
SUBTLE   And the widow?
FACE   No,
Not that I can see. Away!

Exit SUBTLE

64. *conjuring in my circle*: walking 'the round' in the Temple Church, a
circle like that in which the magician would do his conjuring.
69. *firk like a flounder*: a flounder is a small flat-fish.
71. *Verdugo-ship*: a mock title, literally Spanish for hangman.

G

Scene 4

FACE (*to* DAPPER *off-stage*)   Oh sir, you are welcome.

Enter DAPPER

The Doctor is within a-moving for you.
I have had the most ado to win him to it.
He swears you'll be the darling o' the dice.
He never heard her Highness dote till now, he says.   5
Your aunt has giv'n you the most gracious words
That can be thought on.
DAPPER   Shall I see her Grace?
FACE   See her and kiss her too.

Enter DRUGGER *followed by* KASTRIL

                              What? Honest Nab!
Hast brought the damask?
DRUGGER   No, sir, here's tobacco.
FACE   'Tis well done, Nab. Thou'lt bring the damask too?   10
DRUGGER   Yes. Here's the gentleman, Captain, Master Kastril,
I have brought to see the Doctor.
FACE   Where's the widow?
DRUGGER   Sir, as he likes, his sister, he says, shall come.
FACE   Oh, is it so? Good time. Is your name Kastril, sir?
KASTRIL   Ay, and the best o' the Kastrils, I'd be sorry else,   15
By fifteen hundred a year. Where is this doctor?
My mad tobacco boy here tells me of one
That can do things. Has he any skill?
FACE   Wherein, sir?
KASTRIL   To carry a business, manage a quarrel fairly
Upon fit terms.
FACE   It seems, sir, you are but young   20
About the town, that can make that a question!
KASTRIL   Sir, not so young but I have heard some speech
Of the angry boys, and seen 'em take tobacco,
And in his shop, and I can take it too,
And I would fain be one of 'em, and go down   25
And practise in the country.
FACE   Sir, for the duello,

---

19. *carry a business*: manage a duel successfully.
23. *angry boys*: roaring boys, tough, hard-drinking youths in whose society
    there were defined fashions, e.g. in the style and recklessness of tobacco-
    taking.
26. *the duello*: Herford and Simpson refer to the leading authority on this
    subject as *Vincentio Saviolo his Practice. In two books. The first intreating
    of the use of the rapier and dagger. The second of honour and honourable
    quarrels.* 1595.

The Doctor, I assure you, shall inform you
To the least shadow of a hair; and show you
An instrument he has of his own making
Wherewith, no sooner shall you make report   30
Of any quarrel, but he will take the height on't
Most instantly, and tell in what degree
Of safety it lies in, or mortality,
And how it may be borne, whether in a right line
Or a half-circle, or may else be cast   35
Into an angle blunt if not acute.
All this he will demonstrate. And then rules
To give and take the lie by.
KASTRIL   How? To take it?
FACE   Yes, in oblique. He'll show you. Or in circle;
But never in diameter. The whole town   40
Study his theorems and dispute them ordinarily
At the eating academies.
KASTRIL   But does he teach
Living by the wits too?
FACE   Anything whatever.
You cannot think that subtlety but he reads it.
He made me a Captain. I was a stark pimp,   45
Just o' your standing, 'fore I met with him.
It is not two months since. I'll tell you his method.
First he will enter you at some ordinary.
KASTRIL   No, I'll not come there. You shall pardon me.
FACE   For why, sir?
KASTRIL   There's gaming there and tricks.
FACE   Why, would
                                          [you be 50
A gallant and not game?
KASTRIL   Ay, 'twill spend a man.
FACE   Spend you? It will repair you when you are spent.
How do they live by their wits there, that have vented
Six times your fortunes?
KASTRIL   What, three thousand a year!
FACE   Ay, forty thousand.
LASTRIL   Are there such?
FACE   Ay, sir. 55

---

38. *give and take the lie*: how to call your opponent a liar and how to react if
   he calls you one. Cf. Touchstone (*As You Like It*, v, iv).
39. *in oblique*: take the 'lie' as an 'oblique' or hinted attack (so that you can
   escape with some such formula as 'If that had been said in any other words
   I would have had to fight'); or 'in a circle', going a long way round before
   facing the opponent. 'Never in diameter', means never finding yourself
   diammetrically opposed so that fighting is unavoidable.
41. *ordinarily*: at an ordinary, or eating place. For behaviour at the 'eating
   academies' see Dekker's *Gull's Hornbook* Ch. V.

And gallants yet. Here's a young gentleman (*pointing to*
                                              [DAPPER)
Is born to nothing, forty marks a year,
Which I count nothing. He's to be initiated
And have a fly o' the Doctor. He will win you
By unresistible luck within this fortnight   60
Enough to buy a barony. They will set him
Upmost at the groom-porters all the Christmas!
And for the whole year through at every place
Where there is play, present him with the chair,
The best attendance, the best drink, sometimes   65
Two glasses of canary, and pay nothing.
The purest linen, and the sharpest knife,
The partridge next his trencher, and somewhere
The dainty bed in private with the dainty.
You shall ha' your ordinaries bid for him   70
As play-houses for a poet, and the master
Pray him aloud to name what dish he affects,
Which must be buttered shrimps; and those that drink
To no mouth else will drink to his, as being
The goodly president mouth of all the board.   75
KASTRIL   Do you not gull one?
FACE   'Od's my life! Do you think it?
You shall have a cassed commander, can but get
In credit with a glover or a spurrier
For some two pair of either's ware aforehand,
Will, by most swift posts, dealing with him,   80
Arrive at competent means to keep himself,
His punk and naked boy in excellent fashion
And be admired for't.
KASTRIL   Will the Doctor teach this?
FACE   He will do more, sir. When your land is gone
(As men of spirit hate to keep earth long)   85
In a vacation, when small money is stirring,
And ordinaries suspended till the term,
He'll show a perspective where on one side
You shall behold the faces and the persons
Of all sufficient young heirs in town,   90
Whose bonds are current for commodity;

62. *groom-porters*: officers under the Lord Chamberlain. They provided
     equipment for games and gambling in the King's household and had to
     settle disputes that arose out of the play. To be well in with these people,
     especially at Christmas time when there was plenty of gambling going on,
     was an obvious advantage.
66. *canary*: a light sweet wine from the Canary Islands.
70. *ordinaries*: eating houses.
72. *what dish he affects*: 'affects' means 'enjoys', 'has a fancy for'.
77. *cassed*: cashiered.

On th'other side, the merchants' forms, and others,
That without help of any second broker
(Who would expect a share) will trust such parcels;
In the third square, the very street, and sign   95
Where the commodity dwells, and does but wait
To be delivered, be it pepper, soap,
Hops, or tobacco, oat meal, woad or cheeses.
All which you may so handle, to enjoy
To your own use, and never stand obliged.   100
KASTRIL   I'faith! Is he such a fellow?
FACE   Why, Nab here knows
                                                        [him.

And then for making matches for rich widows,
Young gentlewomen, heirs, the fortunat'st man!
He's sent to, far and near, all over England,
To have his counsel and to know their fortunes.   105
KASTRIL   God's will, my suster shall see him!
FACE   I'll tell you, sir,
What he did tell me of Nab. It's a strange thing!
(By the way, you must eat no cheese, Nab: it breeds
                                                        [melancholy
And that same melancholy breeds worms, but pass it).
He told me, honest Nab here was ne'er at tavern   110
But once in's life.
DRUGGER   Truth, and no more I was not.
FACE   And then he was so sick—
DRUGGER   Could he tell you that, too?
FACE   How should I know it?
DRUGGER   In troth, we had been a-shooting,
And had a piece of fat ram-mutton to supper
That lay so heavy o' my stomach—
FACE   And he has no head   115
To bear any wine, for what with the noise o'the fiddlers,
And care of his shop, for he dares keep no servants—
DRUGGER   My head did so ache—
FACE   As he was fain to be brought
                                                        [home,
The Doctor told me. And then a good old woman—
DRUGGER   Yes, faith, she dwells in Seacoal Lane—did cure me   120
With sodden ale and pellitory o' the wall.
Cost me but two-pence. I had another sickness

---

108. *breeds melancholy*: Herford and Simpson quote Burton 'Milk, and all
    that comes of milk, as butter and cheese, curds etc., increase melancholy'
    (*Anatomy of Melancholy* 1, 2, 2, 1.)
121. *pellitory*: a low bushy plant growing on or at the foot of walls. In the
    eighteenth century juice of Pellitory of the Wall was still recommended as
    a medicine.

Was worse than that.

FACE   Ay, that was with the grief
Thou took'st for being 'sessed at eighteen pence
For the water-work.

DRUGGER   In truth, and it was like 125
T'have cost me almost my life.

FACE   Thy hair went off?

DRUGGER Yes, sir, 'twas done for spite.

FACE   Nay, so says the Doctor.

KASTRIL Pray thee, tobacco-boy, go fetch my suster.
I'll see this learned boy before I go,
And so shall she.

FACE   Sir, he is busy now. 130
But if you have a sister to fetch hither,
Perhaps your own pains may command her sooner,
And he by that time will be free.

KASTRIL   I go. (*exit* KASTRIL)

FACE Drugger, she's thine. The damask! (*exit* DRUGGER)
   (*aside*) Subtle and I
Must wrestle for her. Come on, master Dapper, 135
You see how I turn clients here away
To give your case dispatch. Ha' you performed
The ceremonies were enjoined you?

DAPPER   Yes, o' the vinegar
And the clean shirt.

FACE   'Tis well: that shirt may do you
More worship than you think. Your aunt's a-fire, 140
But that she will not show it, t'have a sight on you.
Ha' you provided for her Grace's servants?

DAPPER Yes, here are six-score Edward shillings.

FACE   Good.

DAPPER And an old Harry's sovereign.

FACE   Very good.

DAPPER And three James shillings, and an Elizabethan groat. 145
Just twenty nobles.

FACE   Oh, you are too just.
I would you had had the other noble in Mary's.

DAPPER I have some Philip and Mary's.

FACE   Ay, those same
Are best of all. Where are they? Hark, the Doctor!

---

125. *water-work*: the project for Sir Hugh Middleton's 'new river', was
  begun in 1609 and finished in 1613.
144. *old Harry's sovereign*: ten shillings.

Scene 5

Enter SUBTLE, *disguised like a Priest of Fairy.*

SUBTLE Is yet her Grace's cousin come?

FACE   He is come.

SUBTLE And is he fasting?

FACE   Yes.

SUBTLE And hath cried 'hum'?

FACE (*to* DAPPER) Thrice, you must answer.

DAPPER   Thrice.

SUBTLE   And as oft
                                                  ['buzz'?

FACE If you have, say.

DAPPER   I have.

SUBTLE   Then to her, coz.
  Hoping that he hath vinegared his senses   5
As he was bid, the Fairy Queen dispenses
By me this robe, the petticoat of fortune,
Which that he straight put on she doth importune.
And though to fortune near be her petticoat,
Yet nearer is her smock, the Queen doth note.   10
And therefore, even of that a piece she hath sent
Which, being a child, to wrap him in was rent;
And prays him for a scarf he now will wear it,
With as much love as then her Grace did tear it,
About his eyes (*they blindfold him with a rag*) to show he is
                                                  [fortunate; 15
And trusting unto her to make his state,
He'll throw away all worldly pelf about him;
Which that he will perform she doth not doubt him.

FACE She need not doubt him, sir. Alas, he has nothing
But what he will part withal as willingly   20
Upon her Grace's word (throw away your purse)
As she would ask it (handkerchiefs and all).

    (*he throws away as they bid him*)

  She cannot bid that thing but he'll obey
(If you have a ring about you, cast if off,
Or a silver seal at your wrist—her Grace will send   25
Her fairies here to search you, therefore deal
Directly with her Highness. If they find
That you conceal a mite, you are undone).

DAPPER Truly, there's all.

FACE   All what?

DAPPER   My money, truly.

FACE Keep nothing that is transitory about you.   30

priest of fairy (stage-direction): see Introduction p. 7.
10. *her smock*: an undergarment.

DOL enters with a cittern

(*aside to* SUBTLE) Bid Dol play music. (*to* DAPPER) Look,
the elves are come
To pinch you if you tell not truth. (*they pinch him*) Advise you.

DAPPER   Oh, I have a paper with a spur-ryall in't.

FACE   *Ti, ti,*
They knew't, they say.

SUBTLE   *Ti, ti, ti, ti,* he has more yet.

FACE   *Ti, ti, ti, ti,* I'the t'other pocket?

SUBTLE   *Titi, titi, titi, titi.*   35
They must pinch him or he will never confess, they say.

DAPPER   Oh! Oh!

FACE   Nay, pray you hold: he is her Grace's nephew.
Ti, ti, ti? What care you? Good faith, you shall care.
Deal plainly, sir, and shame the fairies. Show
You are an innocent.

DAPPER   By this good light, I ha' nothing.   40

SUBTLE   *Ti, ti, ti, ti, to, ta.* He does equivocate, she says.
Ti, ti, do, ti, ti, ti, do, ti, da. And swears by the light when he is
                            [blinded. (*exit* DOL)

DAPPER   By this good dark, I ha' nothing but a half-crown
Of gold about my wrist that my love gave me,
And a leaden heart I wore sin' she forsook me.   45

FACE   I thought 'twas something. And would you incur
Your aunt's displeasure for these trifles? Come,
I had rather you had thrown away twenty half-crowns.
You may wear your leaden heart still.

Enter DOL *hastily*

                        How now?

SUBTLE   What news, Dol?

DOL   Yonder's your knight, Sir Mammon! 50

FACE   God's lid, we never thought of him till now!
Where is he?

DOL   Here, hard by. He's at the door.

SUBTLE   And you are not ready now! Dol, get his suit.
He must not be sent back.

FACE   Oh, by no means.
What shall we do with this same puffin here,   55

cittern (stage direction): a kind of lute, popular during the sixteenth and
    seventeenth centuries.
33. *spur-ryall*: The blazing sun on the reverse side of this coin looked like
    a rowel (the wheel with pointed projections at the foot of a spur). The
    value by Jonson's time was 15/-.
55. *puffin*: a bird of the auk family (Face talks of Dapper as being 'on the
    spit'). Also a term of abuse applied to a person puffed up with pride or
    vanity. Dapper is still puffed up with his hopes, though with little else by
    this time.

Now he's o' the spit?
SUBTLE   Why, lay him back awhile
With some device. *Ti, ti, ti, ti, ti.* Would her Grace speak with
                                                    [me?
I come. Help, Dol.

Mammon knocks at the door and FACE *speaks through the keyhole*

FACE   Who's there? Sir Epicure,
My master's i'the way. Please you to walk
Three or four turns, but till his back be turned,   60
And I am for you. Quickly, Dol.
SUBTLE   Her Grace
Commends her kindly to you, master Dapper.
DAPPER   I long to see her Grace.
SUBTLE   She now is set
At dinner, in her bed, and she has sent you,
From her own private trencher, a dead mouse   65
And a piece of gingerbread to be merry withal
And stay your stomach lest you faint with fasting.
Yet if you could hold out till she saw you, she says,
It would be better for you.
FACE   Sir, he shall
Hold out an 'twere this two hours for her Highness,   70
I can assure you that. We will not lose
All we ha' done—
SUBTLE   He must nor see nor speak
To anybody till then.
FACE   For that, we'll put, sir,
A stay in's mouth.
SUBTLE   Of what?
FACE   Of gingerbread.
Make you it fit. (*they gag him*) He that hath pleased her Grace   75
Thus far shall not now crinkle for a little.
(*to* DAPPER) Gape, sir, and let him fit you. (*they thrust a gag of*
                                        [*gingerbread in his mouth*)
SUBTLE   Where shall we now
Bestow him?
DOL   I' the privy.
SUBTLE   Come along, sir,
I now must show you Fortune's privy lodgings.
FACE   Are they perfumed? And his bath ready?
SUBTLE   All.   80
Only the fumigation's somewhat strong.
FACE (*calling*)   Sir Epicure, I am yours, sir, by and by.

Exeunt

76. *crinkle*: shrink back from fulfilling one's purpose.

ACT IV

Scene 1 : *A room in Lovewit's house*

Enter FACE *and* MAMMON

FACE Oh, sir, y'are come i'the only, finest time—
MAMMON Where's master?
FACE   Now preparing for projection, sir.
  Your stuff will be all changed shortly.
MAMMON   Into gold?
FACE To gold and silver, sir.
MAMMON   Silver I care not for.
FACE Yes, sir, a little, to give beggars.
MAMMON   Where's the lady?   5
FACE At hand, here. I ha' told her such brave things o' you,
  Touching your bounty and your noble spirit—
MAMMON   Hast thou?
FACE—As she is almost in her fit to see you.
  But, good sir, no divinity i' your conference,
  For fear of putting her in rage—
MAMMON   I warrant thee.   10
FACE Six men will not hold her down. And then,
  If the old man should hear or see you—
MAMMON   Fear not.
FACE The very house, sir, would run mad. You know it,
  How scrupulous he is and violent
  'Gainst the least act of sin. Physic or mathematics,   15
  Poetry, state or bawdry (as I told you)
  She will endure, and never startle. But
  No word of controversy.
MAMMON   I am schooled, good Ulen.
FACE And you must praise her house, remember that,
  And her nobility.
MAMMON   Let me alone;   20
  No herald, no, nor antiquary, Lungs,
  Shall do it better. Go.
FACE (*aside*)   Why, this is yet
  A kind of modern happiness, to have
  Dol Common for a great lady. (*exit*)
MAMMON   Now, Epicure,
  Heighten thyself: talk to her all in gold;   25
  Rain her as many showers as Jove did drops

18. *controversy*: controversial religious topics.
25. *Heighten*: alchemical term for the process by which base metals were
    elevated.
26. *as many showers as Jove*: Danaë's father imprisoned her in a brass
    chamber: he had learnt that he would be killed by his daughter's son and

Unto his Danaë. Show the God a miser
Compared with Mammon. What? The Stone will do't.
She shall feel gold, taste gold, hear gold, sleep gold:
Nay, we will *concumbere* gold. I will be puissant   30
And mighty in my talk to her! Here she comes.

Re-enter FACE *with* DOL *richly dressed*

FACE   To him, Dol, suckle him. (*aloud*) This is the noble knight
I told your ladyship—
MAMMON   Madam, with your pardon
I kiss your vesture.
DOL   Sir, I were uncivil
If I would suffer that. My lip to you, sir.   35
MAMMON   I hope my lord your brother be in health, lady?
DOL   My lord my brother is, though I no lady, sir.
FACE (*aside*)   Well said, my guinea-bird.
MAMMON   Right noble madam—
FACE (*aside*)   Oh, we shall have most fierce idolatry!
MAMMON   'Tis your prerogative.
DOL   Rather your courtesy.   40
MAMMON   Were there nought else t'enlarge your virtues to me,
These answers speak your breeding and your blood.
DOL   Blood we boast none, sir. A poor baron's daughter.
MAMMON   Poor, and gat you? Profane not! Had your father
Slept all the happy remnant of his life   45
After the act, lien but there still and panted,
He'd done enough to make himself, his issue,
And his posterity noble.
DOL   Sir, although
We may be said to want the gilt and trappings,
The dress of honour, yet we strive to keep   50
The seeds and the materials.
MAMMON   I do see
The old ingredient, virtue, was not lost,
Nor the drug, money, used to make your compound.
There is a strange nobility i' your eye,
This lip, that chin! Methinks you do resemble   55
One o' the Austriac princess.
FACE (*aside*)   Very like!
Her father was an Irish costermonger!
MAMMON   The house of Valois, just, had such a nose,
And such a forehead yet the Medici

intended to make sure that she should never have one. Zeus penetrated
the walls and visited her in a shower of gold. She thus bore a son, Perseus,
who lived to fulfil the prophecy.
30. *concumbere gold*: 'We will make gold when we lie together.'
38. *guinea-bird*: slang for prostitute (cf. *Othello*, I. iii, 314–16).
56. *Austriac*: Austrian.

Of Florence boast.

DOL   Troth, and I have been likened   60
To all these princes.

FACE (*aside*)   I'll be sworn: I heard it.

MAMMON   I know not how, it is not any one
But e'en the very choice of all their features.

FACE (*aside*)   I'll in and laugh. (*exit*)

MAMMON   A certain touch, or air,
That sparkles a divinity beyond   65
An earthly beauty!

DOL   Oh, you play the courtier.

MAMMON   Good lady, gi' me leave—

DOL   In faith, I may not,
To mock me, sir.

MAMMON   To burn i' this sweet flame:
The Phoenix never knew a nobler death.

DOL   Nay, now you court the courtier, and destroy   70
What you would build. This art, sir, i' your words,
Calls your whole faith in question.

MAMMON   By my soul—

DOL   Nay, oaths are made o' the same air, sir.

MAMMON   Nature
Never bestowed upon mortality
A more unblamed, a more harmonious feature.   75
She played the step-dame in all faces else.
Sweet madame, let me be particular—

DOL   Particular, sir? I pray you, know your distance.

MAMMON   In no ill sense, sweet lady; but to ask
How your fair graces pass the hours? I see   80
You are lodged here i' the house of a rare man,
An excellent artist. But what's that to you?

DOL   Yes, sir, I study here the mathematics
And distillation.

MAMMON   Oh, I cry your pardon.
He's a divine instructor! Can extract   85
The souls of all things by his art, call all
The virtues and the miracles of the sun
Into a temperate furnace, teach dull nature
What her own forces are. A man the Emperor
Has courted above Kelly, sent his medals   90

77. *particular*: familiar, specially attentive.
83. *mathematics*: astrology.
84. *distillation*: chemistry.
90. *Kelly*: Edward Kelly (1555–95), a famous alchemist, charlatan and man
    of wit, who collaborated with Dr Dee (see Introduction p. 6). Claimed
    to have discovered the Philosopher's Stone, and later won the favour of
    the Emperor Rudolph in Prague, who became impatient when Kelly
    failed to work any wonders, and put him in prison where he died.

And chains t'invite him.

DOL   Ay, and for his physic, sir—

MAMMON Above the art of Aesculapius,
That drew the envy of the thunderer!
I know all this, and more.

DOL   Troth, I am taken, sir,
Whole with these studies that contemplate nature.   95

MAMMON It is a noble humour. But this form
Was not intended to so dark a use!
Had you been crooked, foul, of some coarse mould,
A cloister had done well. But such a feature
That might stand up the glory of a kingdom,   100
To live recluse is a mere solecism,
Though in a nunnery! It must not be.
I muse my lord your brother will permit it!
You should spend half my land first, were I he.
Does not this diamond better on my finger   105
Than i' the quarry?

DOL   Yes.

MAMMON   Why, you are like it.
You were created, lady, for the light!
Here, you shall wear it. Take it, the first pledge
Of what I speak, to bind you to believe me.

DOL In chains of adamant?

MAMMON   Yes, the strongest bands.   110
And take a secret too. Here by your side
Doth stand, this hour, the happiest man in Europe.

DOL You are contented, sir?

MAMMON   Nay, in true being:
The envy of princes and the fear of states.

DOL Say you so, Sir Epicure?

MAMMON   Yes, and thou shalt prove it,   115
Daughter of honour. I have cast mine eye
Upon thy form, and I will rear this beauty
Above all styles.

DOL   You mean no treason, sir?

MAMMON No, I will take away that jealousy.
I am the lord of the Philosopher's Stone,   120
And thou the lady.

DOL   How, sir? Ha' you that?

MAMMON I am the master of the mystery.
This day the good old wretch here o' the house
Has made it for us. Now he's at projection.
Think therefore thy first wish now; let me hear it.   125

92. *Aesculapius*: Latin form of Asclepius, hero and god of healing. He restored
Hippolytus to life, for which Zeus killed him with a thunderbolt.
101. *solecism*: here something that offends against good sense.

And it shall rain into thy lap no shower
But floods of gold, whole cataracts, a deluge,
To get a nation on thee!
DOL   You are pleased, sir,
To work on the ambition of our sex.
MAMMON   I am pleased the glory of her sex should know   130
This nook here, of the Friars, is no climate
For her to live obscurely in, to learn
Physic and surgery for the constable's wife
Of some odd hundred in Essex. But come forth
And taste the air of palaces. Eat, drink   135
The toils of emprics and their boasted practice;
Tincture of pearl, and coral, gold and amber;
Be seen at feasts and triumphs; have it asked
What miracle she is; set all the eyes
Of court a-fire like a burning glass   140
And work 'em into cinders, when the jewels
Of twenty states adorn thee and the light
Strikes out the stars; that when thy name is mentioned,
Queens may look pale, and, we but showing our love,
Nero's Poppaeia may be lost in story!   145
Thus, will we have it.
DOL   I could well consent, sir.
But in a monarchy, how will this be?
The Prince will soon take notice, and both seize
You and your Stone, it being a wealth unfit
For any private subject.
MAMMON   If he knew it.   150
DOL   Yourself do boast it, sir.
MAMMON   To thee, my life.
DOL   Oh, but beware, sir! You may come to end
The remnant of your days in a loathed prison
By speaking of it.
MAMMON   'Tis no idle fear!
We'll therefore go with all, my girl, and live   155
In a free state, where we will eat our mullets

---

128. *to get a nation*: another reference to the legend of Zeus and Danaë (cf.
   p. 102, l. 26, note). As Zeus came to Danaë in a shower of gold and begat
   the hero Perseus, so the riches that Sir Epicure will shower on Dol will be
   sufficient to give birth to a whole nation.

131. *of the Friars*: at Blackfriars.

136. *toils of emprics*: 'Empric' is a form of 'empiric', usually meaning a
   quack doctor. Mammon is referring respectfully to the alchemists and
   experimenters whom others would see clearly as charlatans. By 'drink the
   toils of emprics', he means 'enjoy the fruits of these wise men's studies'.

145. *Nero's Poppaeia*: a great beauty who became Nero's mistress in A.D. 58
   and his wife four years later.

156. *mullets*: a fish that was a great delicacy in ancient Rome.

Soused in high-country wines, sup pheasants' eggs,
And have our cockles boiled in silver shells,
Our shrimps to swim again, as when they lived,
In a rare butter made of dolphin's milk   160
Whose cream does look like opals. And with these
Delicate meats set ourselves high for pleasure
And take us down again and then renew
Our youth and strength with drinking the elixir
And so enjoy a perpetuity   165
Of life and lust. And thou shalt ha' thy wardrobe
Richer than Nature's, still, to change thyself
And vary oftener for thy pride than she,
Or Art, her wise and almost-equal servant.

Re-enter FACE

FACE   Sir, you are too loud. I hear you, every word,   170
Into the laboratory. Some fitter place:
The garden, or great chamber above. How like you her?
MAMMON   Excellent! Lungs, there's for thee. (*gives him money*)
FACE   But, do you hear,
Good sir, beware, no mention of the rabbins.
MAMMON   We think not on 'em.
FACE   Oh, it is well, sir.   175

Exeunt MAMMON *and* DOL

Scene 2

Subtle!

Enter SUBTLE

Dost thou not laugh?
SUBTLE   Yes. Are they gone?
FACE   All's clear.
SUBTLE   The widow is come.
FACE   And your quarrelling disciple?
SUBTLE   Ay.
FACE   I must to my captainship again then.
SUBTLE   Stay, bring 'em in first.
FACE   So I meant. What is she?
A bonny-bell?
SUBTLE   I know not.
FACE   We'll draw lots.   5
You'll stand to that?
SUBTLE   What else?

157. *high-country*: mountainous.
174. *rabbins*: the chief Jewish authorities on matters of law and doctrine.
  Mention of these writers will throw Dol into her fit.

FACE   Oh, for a suit
To fall now like a curtain, flap!
SUBTLE   To the door, man!
FACE   You'll ha' the first kiss 'cause I am not ready. (*exit*)
SUBTLE   Yes, and perhaps hit you through both the nostrils.
FACE (*off-stage*)   Who would you speak with?
KASTRIL (*off-stage*)   Where's the Captain?
FACE (*off-stage*)   Gone, sir.   10
About some business.
KASTRIL   Gone?
FACE   He'll return straight.
But master Doctor, his lieutenant, is here.
SUBTLE   Come near, my worshipful boy, my *terrae fili*,
That is, my boy of land. Make thy approaches.

Enter KASTRIL *followed by* DAME PLIANT

Welcome, I know thy lusts and thy desires,   15
And I will serve and satisfy 'em. Begin.
Charge me from thence, or thence, or in this line.
Here is my centre. Ground thy quarrel.
KASTRIL   You lie.
SUBTLE   How, child of wrath and anger! The loud lie?
For what, my sudden boy?
KASTRIL   Nay, that look you to,   20
I am afore-hand.
SUBTLE   Oh, this is no true grammar,
And as ill logic! You must render causes, child;
Your first and second intentions, know your canons,
And your divisions, moods, degrees and differences,
Your predicaments, substance, and accident,   25
Series extern and intern, with their causes
Efficient, material, formal, final,
And ha' your elements perfect—
KASTRIL   What, is this
The angry tongue he talks in?
SUBTLE   That false precept
Of being afore-hand has deceived a number   30
And made 'em enter quarrels often-times
Before they were aware, and afterward

6. *oh, for a suit*: Face spends a lot of time changing from one disguise to
another. He now has to get into his Captain's uniform and wishes it could
come down upon him like a curtain.
13. *terrae fili*: literally 'sons of the earth', low-born. Subtle gives a flattering
translation in the next line.
21. *no true grammar*: not according to the rules as enunciated by Saviolo
(cf. p. 94, l. 26, note): 'For to have the lie given lawfully, it is requisite that
the cause whereupon it is given, be particularly specified and declared'
(quoted by Herford and Simpson).

Against their wills.

KASTRIL   How must I do, then, sir?

SUBTLE (*appearing to notice* DAME PLIANT *for the first time*)
I cry this lady mercy! She should first
Have been saluted. I do call you lady   35
Because you are to be one ere't be long,
My soft and buxom widow. (*he kisses her*)

KASTRIL   Is she, i' faith?

SUBTLE   Yes, or my art is an egregious liar.

KASTRIL   How know you?

SUBTLE   By inspection on her forehead
And subtlety of her lip (*he kisses her again*) which must be tasted 40
Often, to make a judgment. 'Slight, she melts
Like a myrobolane! Here is yet a line
In *rivo frontis* tells me he is no knight.

PLIANT   What is he then, sir?

SUBTLE   Let me see your hand.
Oh, your *linea fortunae* makes it plain,   45
And *stella* here *in monte veneris*,
But most of all *junctura annularis*.
He is a soldier or a man of art, lady.
But shall have some great honour shortly.

PLIANT   Brother,
He's a rare man, believe me!

KASTRIL   Hold your peace.   50
Here comes the t'other rare man.

Enter FACE *in his uniform*

                               Save you, Captain.

FACE   Good master Kastril. Is this your sister?

KASTRIL   Ay, sir.
Please you to kuss her, and be proud to know her?

FACE   I shall be proud to know you, lady. (*kisses her*)

PLIANT   Brother,
He calls me lady too.

KASTRIL   Ay, peace. I heard it. (*takes her aside*) 55

FACE (*to* SUBTLE)   The Count is come.

SUBTLE   Where is he?

42. *myrobolane*: a kind of dried Indian plum, recommended as an antidote
    against melancholy.
43. *in rivo frontis*: the frontal vein.
45. *linea fortunae*: the line of fortune, supposed to begin beneath the little
    finger and end under the middle finger.
46. *stella . . . in monte veneris*: literally a star on the mount of Venus, at the
    root or mount of the thumb, revealing amorous disposition if pronounced.
47. *junctura annularis*: the joint of the ring-finger. Subtle is implying that
    Dame Pliant is made for marriage, and therefore for the honour which this
    feature of the hand was reckoned to foretell.

H

FACE   At the door.
SUBTLE   Why, you must entertain him.
FACE   What'll you do
With these the while?
SUBTLE   Why, have 'em up and show 'em
Some fustian book or the dark glass.
FACE   'Fore God,
She is a delicate dab-chick! I must have her.   60
SUBTLE   Must you? Ay, if your fortune will, you must.
(to KASTRIL) Come sir, the Captain will come to us presently.
I'll ha' you to my chamber of demonstrations,
Where I'll show you both the grammar and the logic
And rhetoric of quarrelling: my whole method   65
Drawn out in tables, and my instrument
That hath the several scales upon't shall make you
Able to quarrel at a straw's breadth by moonlight.
And, lady, I'll have you look in a glass
Some half-an-hour, but to clear your eye-sight   70
Against you see your fortune, which is greater
Than I may judge upon the sudden, trust me.

Exeunt

Scene 3

Enter FACE

FACE (*calling*) Where are you, Doctor?
SUBTLE (*off-stage*)   I'll come to you presently.
FACE   I will ha' this same widow, now I ha' seen her,
On any composition.

Enter SUBTLE

SUBTLE   What do you say?
FACE   Ha' you disposed of them?
SUBTLE   I ha' sent 'em up.
FACE   Subtle, in troth, I needs must have this widow.   5
SUBTLE   Is that the matter?
FACE   Nay, but hear me.
SUBTLE   Go to.
If you rebel once, Dol shall know it all.
Therefore be quiet and obey your chance.

---

59. *fustian book*: here something like 'highbrow' or 'egg-head' used as a
    term of abuse. Some old book written in high-flown, bombastic jargon.
60. *dab-chick*: literally, the Little Grebe, a small water-bird.
71. *against you see your fortune*: have her look into the magic crystal so that
    she may see the good fortune that is to be hers.
3. *composition*: meaning 'on any terms'.

FACE   Nay, thou art so violent now—Do but conceive:
Thou art old and canst not serve—
SUBTLE   Who cannot? I?   10
'Slight, I will serve her with thee for a—
FACE   Nay,
But understand: I'll gi' you composition.
SUBTLE   I will not treat with thee. What, sell my fortune?
'Tis better than my birth-right. Do not murmur.
Win her and carry her. If you grumble, Dol   15
Knows it directly.
FACE   Well, sir, I am silent.
Will you go help to fetch in Don, in state? (*exit*)
SUBTLE   I follow you, sir. (*aside*) We must keep Face in awe,
Or he will overlook us like a tyrant.

Re-enter FACE *introducing* SURLY
disguised as a Spaniard

Brain of a tailor, who comes here? Don John?   20
SURLY   *Señores, beso las manos a vuestras mercedes.*
SUBTLE   Would you had stooped a little and kissed our anos.
FACE   Peace, Subtle.
SUBTLE   Stab me, I shall never hold, man.
He looks in that deep ruff like a head in a platter
Served in by a short cloak upon two trestles!   25
FACE   Or what do you say to a collar of brawn, cut down
Beneath the souse and wriggled with a knife?
SUBTLE   'Slud, he does look too fat to be a Spaniard.
FACE   Perhaps some Fleming or some Hollander got him
In d'Alva's time—Count Egmont's bastard.
SUBTLE   Don,   30
Your scurvy, yellow Madrid face is welcome.
SURLY   *Gratia.*
SUBTLE   He speaks out of a fortification.
Pray God he ha' no squibs in those deep sets.
SURLY   *Por dios, Señores, muy linda casa!*

9. *Do but conceive*: 'Just think it out.'
12. *gi' you composition*: 'give you something equal to her in worth'.
14. *murmur*: complain.
20. *Brain of a tailor*: because of Surly's outlandish garb.
21. *Señores* etc.: 'Gentlemen, I kiss your hand.'
27. *souse*: a pig's ears and feet, here the ears.
    wriggled: cut in a wriggly fashion.
29. *Fleming or some Hollander*: the Dutch were proverbially fat and drunken.
30. *In d'Alva's time*: the Duke of Alva (1508–83) became governor-general
    of the Netherlands in 1567, returning to Spain in 1573. He ruthlessly
    crushed the protestants and the patriot leaders, among them Count
    Egmont, executed in 1568.
32. *gratia*: 'thanks'.
33. *squibs . . . sets*: 'no fireworks hidden in the deep folds of his ruff'.

SUBTLE   What says he?

FACE   Praises the house, I think.   35
I know no more but's action.

SUBTLE   Yes, the *casa*,
My precious Diego, will prove fair enough
To cozen you in. Do you mark? You shall
Be cozened, Diego.

FACE   Cozened, do you see,
My worthy Donzel? Cozened.

SURLY   *Entiendo.*   40

SUBTLE   Do you intend it? So do we, dear Don.
Have you brought pistolets? or portugues?
My solemn Don? (FACE *feels in* SURLY'S *pockets*) Dost
                              [thou feel any?

FACE   Full.

SUBTLE   You shall be emptied, Don; pumped and drawn
Dry, as they say.

FACE   Milked, in troth, sweet Don.   45

SUBTLE   See all the monsters; the great lion of all, Don.

SURLY   *Con licencia, se puede ver a esta Señora?*

SUBTLE   What talks he now?

FACE   O' the Señora.

SUBTLE   Oh Don,
That is the lioness which you shall see
Also, my Don.

FACE   'Slid, Subtle, how shall we do?   50

SUBTLE   For what?

FACE   Why, Dol's employed, you know.

SUBTLE   That's true!
'Fore Heaven, I know not. He must stay, that's all.

FACE   Stay? That he must not by no means.

SUBTLE   No? Why?

FACE   Unless you'll mar all. 'Slight, he'll suspect it.
And then he will not pay, not half so well.   55
This is a travelled punk-master, and does know
All the delays; a notable hot rascal
And looks already rampant.

SUBTLE   'Sdeath, and Mammon
Must not be troubled.

FACE   Mammon, in no case.

SUBTLE   What shall we do then?

FACE   Think: you must be
                              [sudden.   60

---

34. *Por dios* etc.: 'By God, gentlemen, a very handsome house!'
40. *Entiendo*: 'I hear' (i.e. understand).
47. *con licencia*: 'With your permission, can I see this lady?'

SURLY *Entiendo que la Señora es tan hermosa, que codicio tan*
a verla, como la bien aventuranca de mi vida.

FACE *Mi vida?* 'Slid, Subtle, he puts me in mind o' the widow.
What dost thou say to draw her to it, ha?
And tell her it is her fortune? All our venture   65
Now lies upon't. It is but one man more
Which on's chance to have her, and beside
There is no maidenhead to be feared or lost.
What dost thou think on't, Subtle?

SUBTLE   Who, I? Why—

FACE   The credit of our house too is engaged.   70

SUBTLE   You made me an offer for my share e'rewhile.
What wilt thou gi' me, i'faith?

FACE   Oh, by that light,
I'll not buy now. You know your doom to me.
E'en take your lot, obey your chance, sir. Win her
And wear her out, for me.

SUBTLE   'Slight. I'll not work her then.   75

FACE   It is the common cause. Therefore bethink you.
Dol else must know it, as you said.

SUBTLE   I care not.

SURLY *Señores, por que se tarda tanta?*

SUBTLE   Faith, I am not fit. I am old.

FACE   That's now no reason, sir.

SURLY *Puede ser, de hazer burla de mi amor?*   80

FACE   You hear the Don too? By this air, I call,
And loose the hinges. (*calls*) Dol!

SUBTLE   A plague of hell—

FACE   Will you then do?

SUBTLE   You are a terrible rogue!
I'll think of this. Will you, sir, call the widow?

FACE   Yes, and I'll take her too, with all her faults,   85
Now I do think on't better.

SUBTLE   With all my heart, sir.
Am I discharged o' the lot?

FACE   As you please.

SUBTLE   Hands. (*they shake
                              [hands*)

FACE   Remember now, that upon any change
You never claim her.

SUBTLE   Much good joy and health to you, sir.

---

61. *Entiendo que.* . . . etc.: 'I hear that the lady is so beautiful that I want
greatly to see her as the great good fortune of my life.'
78. *Señores, por que*: 'Gentlemen, why so much delay?'
80. *puede ser* etc.: 'Can you be mocking my love?'
82. *loose the hinges*: 'risk the whole thing falling apart'.
87. *discharged o' the lot*: 'Am I freed from having to take my share in the
gamble?'

Marry a whore? Fate, let me wed a witch first.   90
SURLY   *Por estas honradas barbas—*
SUBTLE   He swears by his beard.
Dispatch, and call the brother too. (*exit* FACE)
SURLY   *Tiengo duda, Señores,*
Que on me hagan alguna traycion.
SUBTLE   How? Issue on? Yes, presto, Señor. Please you
Enthratha the *chambratha*, worthy Don;   95
Where, if it please the Fates, in your *bathada*
You shall be soaked and stroked and tubbed and rubbed,
And scrubbed and fubbed, dear Don, before you go.
You shall, in faith, my scurvy baboon Don,
Be curried, clawed and flawed and tawed, indeed.   100
I will the heartlier go about it now,
And make the widow a punk so much the sooner
To be revenged on this impetuous Face.
The quickly doing of it is the grace.

Exeunt SUBTLE *and* SURLY

Scene 4: *Another room in the same*

Enter FACE, KASTRIL *and* DAME PLIANT

FACE   Come, lady. I knew the Doctor would not leave
Till he had found the very nick of her fortune.
KASTRIL   To be a countess, say you?
FACE   A Spanish countess, sir.
PLIANT   Why, is that better than an English countess?
FACE   Better? 'Slight, make you that a question, lady?   5
KASTRIL   Nay, she is a fool, Captain. You must pardon her.
FACE   Ask from your courtier to your inns-of-court man
To your mere milliner. They will tell you all,
Your Spanish jennet is the best horse. Your Spanish
Stoop is the best garb. Your Spanish beard   10
Is the best cut. Your Spanish ruffs are the best
Wear. Your Spanish Pavan the best dance.

91.   *Por estas honradas*: 'By this honoured beard—'.
92.   *Tiengo duda* etc.: 'I am afraid, gentlemen, that you are playing some trick upon me.'
94.   *Issue on*: parodying the sound of the Spanish 'traycion'.
98.   *fubbed*: deceived, put off deceitfully.
100.   *flawed*: flayed.
        tawed: leather was 'tawed' with alum to make it supple.
9.   *jennet*: a small Spanish breed of horse.
10.   *stoop*: presumably some part of Spanish dress, yet 'stoop' does not seem to have a meaning that would fit this. It could mean ceremonial bowing; so Face may be saying that the Spaniard is the most courtly and graceful in his manner.

Your Spanish titillation in a glove
The best perfume. And, for your Spanish pike,
And Spanish blade, let your poor Captain speak.   15
Here comes the Doctor.

Enter SUBTLE *with a scroll.*

SUBTLE   My most honoured lady,
For so I am now to style you, having found
By this my scheme you are to undergo
An honourable fortune very shortly:
What will you say now if some—
FACE   I ha' told her all, sir,   20
And her right worshipful brother here, that she shall be
A countess. Do not delay 'em, sir. A Spanish countess.
SUBTLE   Still, my scarce worshipful Captain, you can keep
No secret. Well, since he has told you, madam,
Do you forgive him, and I do.
KASTRIL   She shall do that, sir.   25
I'll look to't, 'tis my charge.
SUBTLE   Well then, nought rests
But that she fit her love, now, to her fortune.
PLIANT   Truly, I shall never brook a Spaniard.
SUBTLE   No?
PLIANT   Never sin' 'eighty-eight could I abide 'em.
And that was some three year afore I was born, in truth.   30
SUBTLE   Come, you must love him or be miserable.
Choose which you will.
FACE   By this good rush, persuade her.
She will cry strawberries else within this twelve-month.
SUBTLE   Nay, shads and mackerel, which is worse.
FACE   Indeed, sir.
KASTRIL   God's lid, you shall love him or I'll kick you!   35
PLIANT   Why, I'll do as you will ha' me, brother.
KASTRIL   Do,
Or, by this hand, I'll maul you.
FACE   Nay, good sir,
Be not so fierce.
SUBTLE   No, my enraged child,
She will be ruled. What, when she comes to taste
The pleasures of a countess! To be courted—   40

13. *titillation*: perfume. Spanish gloves were perfumed in an elaborate
    fashion: flowers, wine, oils and spices were all involved in the preparation,
    and after five immersions the scent was irremovable.
28. *brook*: put up with, endure.
29. *'eighty-eight*: 1588, year of the Armada (making Dame Pliant nineteen
    years old in 1610, the year of the play).
32. *by this good rush*: floors were still commonly strewn with rushes.
33. *cry strawberries*: be on the streets crying her wares.
34. *shads and mackerel*: be a fish-wife of Billingsgate.

FACE   And kissed and ruffled!
SUBTLE   Ay, behind the hangings.
FACE   And then come forth in pomp!
SUBTLE   And know her state!
FACE   Of keeping all th'idolators o' the chamber
Barer to her than at their prayers!
SUBTLE   Is served
Upon the knee!
FACE   And has her pages, ushers,   45
Footmen and coaches—
SUBTLE   Her six mares—
FACE   Nay, eight—
SUBTLE   To hurry her through London to th' Exchange,
Bethlem, the china-houses—
FACE   Yes, and have
The citizens gape at her and praise her tires!
And my lord's goose-turd bands that rides with her!   50
KASTRIL   Most brave? By this hand, you are not my suster
If you refuse.
PLIANT   I will not refuse, brother.

                    Enter SURLY

SURLY   *Que es esto, Señores, que non se venga?*
Esta tardanza me mata!
FACE   It is the Count come!
The Doctor knew he would be here, by his art.   55
SUBTLE   *En gallanta madama, Don! Gallantissima!*
SURLY   *Por todos los dioses, la mas acabada*
Hermosura que he visto en mi vida!
FACE   Is't not a gallant language that they speak?
KASTRIL   An admirable language! Is't not French?   60
FACE   No. Spanish, sir.
KASTRIL   It goes like law-French,
And that, they say, is the courtliest language.
FACE   List, sir.
SURLY   *El sol ha perdido su lumbre, con el*
Resplandor que trae esta dama. Valgame dios!

47. *Exchange*: the New Exchange in the Strand, 'Britain's Burse', built
    1608–9 with milliners' and sempstresses' shops.
48. *Bethlem*: old form of Bedlam, the lunatic asylum originally in Bishops-
    gate. A trip to see the mad folk was considered an amusement.
50. *goose-turd bands*: yellow-green bands from the collar.
53. *Que es esto* etc.: 'How is this, gentlemen, that she does not come?'
54. *Esta tardanza* etc. (same speech): 'This delay is killing me'.
56. *En gallanta* etc.: 'A fine lady, Don! Most fine!'
57–58. *Por todos* etc.: 'By all the gods, the most perfect beauty that I have
    seen in my life!'
63–64. *El sol* etc.: 'The sun has lost its light, with the splendour which this
    lady brings. God bless me!'

FACE   He admires your sister.

KASTRIL   Must not she make curtsey?   65

SUBTLE   'Ods will, she must go to him, man, and kiss him!
It is the Spanish fashion for the women
To make first court.

FACE   'Tis true he tells you, sir.
His art knows all.

SURLY   *Per que no se acude?*

KASTRIL   He speaks to her, I think?

FACE   That he does, sir.   70

SURLY   *Por el amor de dios, que es esto, que se tarda?*

KASTRIL   Nay, see! She will not understand him! Gull!
Noddy!

PLIANT   What say you, brother?

KASTRIL   Ass, my suster,
Go kuss him as the cunning man would ha' you.
I'll thrust a pin i' your buttocks else.

FACE   Oh no, sir.   75

SURLY   *Señora mia, mi persona muy indigna esta*
A llegar a tanta hermosura.

FACE   Does he not use her bravely?

KASTRIL   Bravely, i'faith!

FACE   Nay, he will use her better.

KASTRIL   Do you think so?

SURLY   *Señora, si sera servida, entremos.* (*leads* PLIANT *out*)   80

KASTRIL   Where does he carry her?

FACE   Into the garden, sir.
Take you no thought. I must interpret for her.

SUBTLE   (*aside to* FACE) Give Dol the word.

Exit FACE

(*to* KASTRIL) Come, my fierce child, advance.
We'll to our quarrelling lesson again.

KASTRIL   Agreed.
I love a Spanish boy, with all my heart.   85

SUBTLE   Nay, and by this means, sir, you shall be brother
To a great Count.

KASTRIL   Ay, I knew that at first.
This match will advance the house of the Kastrils.

SUBTLE   Pray God your sister prove but pliant.

KASTRIL   Why,
Her name is so: by her other husband.

69. *Per que* etc.: 'Why does she not come to me?'
71. *Por el amor* etc.: 'For the love of God, why is this that she delays?'
76. *Señora mia*: 'My lady, my person is very unworthy to approach such
   great beauty.'
78. *bravely*: in fine courtly style.
80. *Señora, si sera* etc.: 'Lady, if it suits you, let us enter.'

SUBTLE   How?   90
KASTRIL   The widow Pliant. Knew you not that?
SUBTLE   No faith, sir.
  Yet by erection of her figure, I guessed it.
  Come, let's go practise.
KASTRIL   Yes, but do you think, Doctor,
  I e'er shall quarrel well?
SUBTLE   I warrant you.

Exeunt

Scene 5: Another room in Lovewit's house

Enter DOL *in her fit of raving, followed by* MAMMON

DOL   For after Alexander's death—
MAMMON   Good lady—
DOL   That Perdicas and Antigonus were slain,
  The two that stood, Seleuce and Ptolemy—
MAMMON   Madam!
DOL   Made up the two legs, and the fourth beast,
  That was Gog-north and Egypt-south, which after   5
  Was called Gog-Iron-leg and South-Iron-leg—
MAMMON   Lady—
DOL   And then Gog-horned. So was Egypt too.
  Then Egypt-clay-leg and Gog-clay-leg—
MAMMON   Sweet madam!
DOL   And last Gog-dust and Egypt-dust, which fall
  In the last link of the fourth chain. And these   10
  Be stars in story, which none see or look at—
MAMMON   What shall I do?
DOL   For, as he says, except
  We call the rabbins and the heathen Greeks—
MAMMON   Dear lady!
DOL   To come from Salem and from Athens

92. *erection of her figure*: casting her horoscope.
    her fit of raving (stage-direction): Dol's 'raving' is a parody of the writings
    of Hugh Broughton (1549–1612), a distinguished Hebrew scholar and the
    author of *A Concent of Scripture* (1588) in which he attempted to settle the
    chronology of the Bible. Jonson has another laugh at his expense in
    Volpone (II, ii, 117).
  2. *Perdicas and Antigonus*: The Empire of Alexander the Great was divided
    among four men, Perdicas and Antigonus being killed by Seleucus and
    Ptolemy.
  5. *Gog-north*: In *A Concent of Scripture*, Broughton uses these terms as
    headings for the columns of his divisions. 'Gog' was also in Elizabethan
    language a corruption of 'God' used in oaths.
  10. *the fourth chain*: Broughton sees history as divided into four 'chains' or
    periods.
  11. *stars in story*: a quotation from Broughton referring to the Jews and
    Greeks who bore witness to Christ.
  14–15. *Salem . . . Athens* etc.: Herford and Simpson quote from *A Consent*

And teach the people of Great Britain—

Enter FACE

FACE   What's the matter, sir?   15
DOL   To speak the tongue of Eber and Javan—
MAMMON   Oh,
She's in her fit!
DOL   We shall know nothing—
FACE   Death, sir.
We are undone!
DOL   Where then a learned linguist
Shall see the ancient used communion
Of vowels and consonants—
FACE   My Master will hear!   20
DOL   A wisdom which Pythagoras held most high—
MAMMON   Sweet honorable lady!
DOL   To comprise
All sounds of voices in few marks of letters—
FACE   Nay, you must never hope to lay her now.
(they speak together)

DOL And so we may arrive by	FACE How did you put her into't?
Talmud skill	MAMMON Alas, I talked 25
And profane Greek to raise the building up	Of a fifth monarchy I would erect
Of Heber's house against the Ismaelite,	With the Philosopher's Stone by chance, and she
King of Thogarma and his habergeons	Falls on the other four straight. FACE Out of Broughton.

of Scripture: 'For this work I endeavoured to call ancient Ebrews and
Greeks to further the building of justice and peace, to come from Salem
and Athens, to these ends of the earth, the possession of Christ: to speak in
England the tongues of Eber and Javan' (i.e. Hebrew and Greek).

19–22. *ancient used communion* etc.: satire again directed against mystical
divines, especially a work called *The Preface of the Families sprung from
Noah's near Posterity*. What follows, where Dol, Face and Mammon all
speak together, is in the jargon of the divinity scholars with references to
Ezekiel, the Book of Revelation, and early learned writers.

25. *Talmud skill*: The Talmud is the great collection of rabbinical teachings
developed from the Old Testament during the second, fourth and sixth
centuries.

26. *fifth monarchy*: 'Fifth Monarchy Men' believed that Christ's second
coming was imminent (his kingdom would then follow those of Assyria,
Persia, Greece and Rome).

28. *Thogarma*: 'Gomer and all his bands: the house of Togarmah of the
north quarters, and all his bands: and many people with thee' (Ezekiel,
xxxviii, 6). These were some of the forces who were to support Ezekiel
against Gog, the chief prince of Meshech and Tubal.
habergeons: a sleeveless coat of armour. That makes no sense here, but
Dol is more concerned with the sound of the thing.

Brimstony, blue and fiery, and the force
Of King Abaddon and the beast of Cittim,
Which Rabbi David Kimchi, Onkelos,
And Aben-Ezra do interpret Rome.

I told you so. 'Slid, stop her mouth. MAMMON Is't best?
FACE She'll never leave else.
If the old man hear her   30
We are but faeces, ashes.
SUBTLE (*off-stage*) What's to do there?
FACE Oh, we are lost. Now she hears him she is quiet.

SUBTLE *enters and they run different ways*

MAMMON Where shall I hide me?
SUBTLE   How? What sight is here?
Close deeds of darkness and that shun the light!
Bring him again! Who is he? What, my son?
Oh, I have lived too long! (*exit* FACE *unobserved*)   35
MAMMON   Nay, good, dear father,
There was no unchaste purpose.
SUBTLE   Not? And flee me
When I come in?
MAMMON   That was my error.
SUBTLE   Error?
Guilt! Guilt, my son. Give it the right name. No marvel
If I found check in our great work within,   40
When such affairs as these were managing!
MAMMON Why, have you so?
SUBTLE   It has stood still this half-hour,
And all the rest of our less work's gone back.
Where is the instrument of wickedness,
My lewd, false drudge?
MAMMON   Nay, good sir, blame not him.   45
Believe me, 'twas against his will or knowledge.
I saw her by chance.
SUBTLE   Will you commit more sin
T''excuse a varlet?
MAMMON   By my hope, 'tis true, sir.
SUBTLE Nay then, I wonder less if you, for whom
The blessing was prepared, would so tempt heaven   50
And lose your fortunes.
MAMMON   Why, sir?
SUBTLE   This'll retard
The work a month at least.

---

30. *King Abaddon and the beast of Cittim*: the Pope. Broughton lists 'King of Locusts, Abaddon, Apollyon' as all 'an excellent name of the Pope'.
31. *David Kimchi*: 1160–1235. Hebrew scholar.
  Onkelos: scholar of the first century.
32. *Aben-Ezra*: divinity scholar and poet (1092–1167).

MAMMON   Why, if it do,
What remedy? But think it not, good father:
Our purposes were honest.
SUBTLE   As they were,
So the reward will prove. (*a great crack and
noise is heard*) How now! Ay me!   55
God and all saints be good to us!

Enter FACE

                    What's that?
FACE   Oh sir, we are defeated! All the works
Are flown *in fumo*. Every glass is burst.
Furnace and all rent down! As if a bolt
Of thunder had been driven through the house.   60
Retorts, receivers, pelicans, bolt-heads,
All struck in shivers! (SUBTLE *falls down as if in a swoon*)
                    Help, good sir! Alas,
Coldness and death invades him. Nay, Sir Mammon,
Do the fair offices of a man! You stand
As you were readier to depart than he. (*knocking heard*)   65
Who's there? My lord her brother is come.
MAMMON   Ha, Lungs?
FACE   His coach is at the door. Avoid his sight,
For he's as furious as his sister is mad.
MAMMON   Alas!
FACE   My brain is quite undone with the fume, sir.
I ne'er must hope to be mine own man again.   70
MAMMON   Is all lost, Lungs? Will nothing be preserved
Of all our cost?
FACE   Faith, very little, sir.
A peck of coals or so, which is cold comfort, sir.
MAMMON   Oh, my voluptuous mind! I am justly punished.
FACE   And so am I, sir.
MAMMON   Cast from all my hopes—   75
FACE   Nay, certainties, sir.
MAMMON   By mine own base affections.
SUBTLE (*seeming to come to himself*)   Oh, the cursed fruits of
                                        [vice and lust!
MAMMON   Good father,
It was my sin. Forgive it.
SUBTLE   Hangs my roof
Over us still and will not fall? Oh justice
Upon us for this wicked man!
FACE (*to* MAMMON)   Nay, look, sir,   80

58. *in fumo*: in vapour (cf. the last line of 'The Argument' and the note on
    this).

You grieve him now with staying in his sight.
Good sir, the nobleman will come too and take you,
And that may breed a tragedy.
MAMMON   I'll go.
FACE   Ay, and repent at home, sir. It may be
For some good penance you may ha' it yet: 85
A hundred pound to the box at Bethlem—
MAMMON   Yes.
FACE   For the restoring such as ha' their wits.
MAMMON   I'll do't.
FACE   I'll send one to you to receive it.
MAMMON   Do.
Is no projection left?
FACE   All flown or stinks, sir.
MAMMON   Will nought be saved that's good for medicine,
                                        [thinkst thou? 90
FACE   I cannot tell, sir. There will be, perhaps,
Something about the scraping of the shards
Will cure the itch, though not your itch of mind, sir.
It shall be saved for you and sent home. Good sir,
This way, for fear the lord should meet you.   95

FACE *shows* SIR MAMMON *out*

SUBTLE (*getting up*)   Face!
FACE   Ay.
SUBTLE   Is he gone?
FACE   Yes, and as heavily
As all the gold he hoped for were in his blood.
Let us be light, though.
SUBTLE   Ay, as balls, and bound
And hit our heads against the roof for joy.
There's so much of our care now cast away.   100
FACE   Now to our Don.
SUBTLE   Yes, your young widow by this time
Is made a countess, Face. She's been in travail
Of a young heir for you.
FACE   Good, sir.
SUBTLE   Off with your case,
And greet her kindly as a bridegroom should   105
After these common hazards.
FACE   Very well, sir.
Will you go fetch Don Diego off the while?
SUBTLE   And fetch him over too, if you'll be pleased, sir.

86. *Bethlem*: Bedlam, the lunatic asylum (cf. p. 116, l. 48, note).
92. *shards*: pieces of broken crockery.
104. *off with your case*: that is, with his disguise as 'Lungs', the alchemist's
    assistant.

Would Dol were in her place, to pick his pockets now!
FACE Why, you can do it as well, if you would set to't.   110
I pray you prove your virtue.
SUBTLE   For your sake, sir.

Exeunt

Scene 6: Another room in the same

Enter SURLY *and* DAME PLIANT

SURLY Lady, you see into what hands you are fallen,
'Mongst what a nest of villains, and how near
Your honour was t'have catched a certain clap
Through your credulity had I but been,
So punctually forward as place, time,   5
And other circumstance would ha' made a man,
For you're a handsome woman. Would you were wise, too.
I am a gentleman, come here disguised,
Only to find the knaveries of this citadel,
And where I might have wronged your honour and have not,   10
I claim some interest in your love. You are,
They say, a widow, rich, and I am a bachelor,
Worth nought. Your fortunes may make me a man,
As mine ha' preserved you a woman. Think upon it,
And whether I have deserved you or no.
PLIANT   I will, sir.   15
SURLY And for these household rogues, let me alone
To treat with them.

Enter SUBTLE

SUBTLE   How doth my noble Diego?
And my dear madam Countess? Hath the count
Been courteous, lady? Liberal and open?
Donzell, methinks you look melancholic   20
After your coitum, and scurvy! Truly
I do not like the dullness of your eye.
It hath a heavy cast, 'tis upsee Dutch,
And says you are a lumpish whore-master.
Be lighter. I will make your pockets so. (*He starts to pick them*) 25
SURLY Will you, Don-bawd and pick-purse? How now? Reel
                                                          [you?

---

20. *melancholic*: 'Omne animal post coitum triste est'. 'Scurvy' goes with
'melancholic', both adjectives to describe Surly's appearance.
23. *upsee Dutch*: meaning heavy, phlegmatic. The Dutch were thought of as
fat, dull creatures, eating and drinking heavily. 'Upsee' derives from the
Dutch 'op zijn' (cf., 'Drink me upsey-Dutch. Frolic and fear not'. *Beggar's
Bush*, III, 3). Cf. also p. 111, l. 29, note.

Stand up, sir! You shall find since I am so heavy
I'll gi' you equal weight. (*starts to beat* SUBTLE)
SUBTLE   Help, murder!
SURLY   No, sir.
There's no such thing intended. A good cart
And a clean whip shall ease you of that fear.   30
I am the Spanish Don that should be cozened,
Do you see? Cozened. Where's your Captain Face?
That parcel-broker and whole-bawd, all rascal?

Enter FACE *in his uniform*

FACE   How, Surly!
SURLY   Oh, make your approach, good Captain.
I have found from whence your copper rings and spoons   35
Come now, wherewith you cheat abroad in taverns.
'Twas here you learned to anoint your boot with brimstone
Then rub men's gold on't for a kind of touch
And say 'twas nought when you had changed the colour
That you might ha't for nothing? And this Doctor,   40
Your sooty, smoky-bearded compeer, he
Will close you so much gold in a bolt's head
And on a turn convey i'the stead another
With sublimed mercury that shall burst i' the heat
And fly out all *in fumo*. Then weeps Mammon,   45
Then swoons his worship. Or he is the Faustus (FACE *slips out*)
That casteth figures and can conjure, cures
Plague, piles and pox, by the ephemerides,
And holds intelligence with all the bawds
And midwives of three shires. While you send in—   50
Captain—what, is he gone? damsels with child,
Wives that are barren, or the waiting maid
With the green sickness (*seizes* SUBTLE *as he is creeping out*)
                                        [Nay, sir, you must tarry
Though he be 'scaped, and answer by the ears, sir.

29–30. *A good cart*: Surly intends to hand him over to justice where his
penalty will be to ride through the streets being pelted by the people, and
then to be whipped.
33. *parcel*: part.
46. *Faustus*: Jonson's contemporaries knew all about him, partly from
Marlowe's play, partly from the Faustbook, a popular collection of tales
about Faustus' conjuring tricks, as well as the story of the sale of his soul
to the devil. By 'casteth figures', Surly means he could set a horoscope and
tell fortunes. 'Cures plague' is another reference to Faustus, cf. Marlowe:

> Are not thy bills hung up as monuments,
> Whereby whole cities have escaped the plague?   (48–9)

48. *by the ephemerides*: a set of tables showing the position of the heavenly
bodies at different times of day.
54. *by the ears*: perhaps he has caught Subtle by the ears; also one of the
punishments of the law was mutilation, such as cutting off the ears.

Scene 7

Re-enter FACE *with* KASTRIL

FACE (*to* KASTRIL)　Why, now's the time, if ever you will quarrel
Well, as they say, and be a true-born child.
The Doctor and your sister both are abused.
KASTRIL　Where is he? Which is he? He is a slave,
Whate'er he is, and the son of a whore. Are you　　　　5
The man, sir, I would know? (*to* SURLY)
SURLY　　　　　　　　I should be loth, sir,
To confess so much.
KASTRIL　　　　　Then you lie i' your throat.
SURLY　　　　　　　　　　How?
FACE (*to* KASTRIL)　A very errant rogue, sir, and a cheater,
Employed here by another conjurer
That does not love the Doctor and would cross him　　　10
If he knew how—
SURLY (*to* KASTRIL)　Sir, you are abused.
KASTRIL　　　　　　　　　　You lie,
And 'tis no matter.
FACE　　　　　Well said, sir. He is
The impudent'st rascal—
SURLY　　　　　　You are indeed. Will you hear me, sir?
FACE　By no means. Bid him be gone.
KASTRIL　　　　　　　　Be gone, sir, quickly.
SURLY　This is strange! Lady, do you inform your brother.　　　15
FACE　There is not such a foist in all the town.
The Doctor had him presently and finds yet
The Spanish Count will come here. Bear up, Subtle. (*aside*)
SUBTLE　Yes, sir, he must appear within this hour.
FACE　And yet this rogue would come in a disguise,　　　20
By the temptation of another spirit,
To trouble our art, though he could not hurt it.
KASTRIL　　　　　　　　　　　Ay.
I know—(*to* PLIANT) Away! You talk like a foolish mauther.
SURLY　Sir, all is truth she says.
FACE　　　　　　　　Do not believe him, sir.
He is the lying'st swabber! Come your ways, sir.　　　25

11–12. *You lie, and 'tis no matter*: Kastril has learnt one law of quarrelling
—to give the lie impressively and then retract it with some 'covering'
expression.

16. *foist*: cheat (literally a term in dice-play, where the cheat may hide the
dice in his palm).

23. *mauther*: a young girl, green, inexperienced and awkward. An East
Anglian word suitable for Kastril's provincial manner.

25. *swabber*: term of contempt (one who swabs a deck).

I

SURLY   You are valiant out of company.

KASTRIL   Yes, how then, sir?

Enter DRUGGER *with a piece of damask*

FACE   Nay, here's an honest fellow, too, that knows him
And all his tricks. (*aside*) Make good what I say, Abel.
This cheater would ha' cozened thee o' the widow.
(*aloud*) He owes this honest Drugger here seven pound   30
He has had on him in two penny'orths of tobacco.

DRUGGER   Yes, sir. And he has damned himself three terms to
                                                    [pay me.

FACE   And what does he owe for lotium?

DRUGGER   Thirty shillings, sir;
And for six syringes.

SURLY   Hydra of villainy!

FACE   Nay, sir, you must quarrel him out o'the house.

KASTRIL   I will.   35
Sir, if you get not out o'doors, you lie,
And you are a pimp.

SURLY   Why, this is madness, sir,
Not valour in you. I must laugh at this.

KASTRIL   It is my humour. You are a pimp and a trig,
And an *Amadis de Gaule* or a *Don Quixote*.   40

DRUGGER   Or a knight o' the curious coxcomb. Do you see?

Enter ANANIAS

ANANIAS.   Peace be to this household.

KASTRIL   I'll keep peace for no man.

ANANIAS   Casting of dollars is concluded lawful.

KASTRIL   Is he the Constable?

SUBTLE   Peace, Ananias.

FACE   No, sir.

KASTRIL   Then you are an otter and a shad, a whit,   45

---

33. *lotium*: 'stale urine used by barbers as a "lye" for the hair' (*O.E.D.*).
34. *syringes*: instruments for squirting.
    Hydra: the many-headed monster whose heads grew again twice as fast as
    Hercules cut them off.
39. *trig*: literally 'a trim, spruce fellow'. Here a term of abuse, 'a dandy, a
    coxcomb' (*O.E.D*).
40. *Amadis de Gaule*: a Spanish or Portuguese romance printed early in the
    16th century, derived from mediaeval tales. Jonson despised it and *Don
    Quixote*, published in 1605. Drugger's remark, capping Kastril's, refers to
    Quixote, implying that the 'Don' looks absurd in his extravagant head-
    gear (the 'lewd hat' that Ananias is to refer to later).
45–46. *an otter* etc.: Falstaff calls Mistress Quickly an otter (*Henry IV, Part
    I*, III, iii) because 'she's neither fish nor flesh'. A shad is a herring, and
    common. *Whit*: a slang term; a bawd in *Bartholomew Fair* is called Cap-
    tain Whit (generally it meant 'a very little', 'a small extent'). Meaning of
    tim unknown.

A very tim.

SURLY　　　You'll hear me, sir?

KASTRIL　　　　　　　I will not.

ANANIAS　What is the motive?

SUBTLE　　　　　　　　　Zeal in the young gentleman
Against his Spanish slops—

ANANIAS　　　　　　They are profane,
Lewd, superstitious, and idolatrous breeches.

SURLY　New rascals!

KASTRIL　　　　　　　Will you be gone, sir?

ANANIAS　　　　　　　　　Avoid, Satan!　　50
Thou art not of the light. That ruff of pride
About thy neck betrays thee, and is the same
With that which the unclean birds in 'seventy-seven
Were seen to prank it with on divers coasts.
Thou look'st like Antichrist in that lewd hat.　　55

SURLY　I must give way.

KASTRIL　　　　　　　Be gone, sir.

SURLY　　　　　　　　　But I'll take
A course with you—

ANANIAS　　　　　Depart, proud Spanish fiend.

SURLY　Captain and Doctor—

ANANIAS　　　　　　　Child of perdition!

KASTRIL　　　　　　　　　　Hence, sir!

Exit SURLY

(*to* FACE) Did I not quarrel bravely?

FACE　　　　　　　　　Yes, indeed, sir.

KASTRIL　Nay, and I give my mind to it. I shall do't.　　60

FACE　Oh, you must follow, sir, and threaten him tame.
He'll turn again else.

KASTRIL　　　　　I'll re-turn him, then. (*exit*)

FACE　Drugger, this rogue prevented us for thee.
We had determined that thou shouldst ha' come
In a Spanish suit and ha' carried her so; and he,　　65
A brokerly slave, goes, puts it on himself.
Hast brought the damask?

DRUGGER　　　　　Yes, sir.

---

53. *unclean birds in 'seventy-seven*: 1577 was the date of D'Alva's invasion of
the Netherlands and crushing of the protestants. Ananias is characteris-
tically using biblical language. Cf.: 'And he cried mightily with a strong
voice, saying, Babylon the great is fallen, is fallen, and is become the habita-
tion of devils, and the hold of every foul spirit, and a cage of every unclean
and hateful bird.' (Revelation xviii, 2).

54. *prank it with*: showing off their fancy, foppish dress.

61. *threaten him tame*: follow him with taunts until you have quite tamed
him.

63. *prevented*: anticipated.

FACE   Thou must borrow
A Spanish suit. Hast thou no credit with the players?
DRUGGER Yes, sir. Did you never see me play the fool?
FACE I know not, Nab. Thou shalt, if I can help it.   70
Hieronymo's old cloak, ruff and hat will serve.
I'll tell thee more when thou bring'st 'em. (*exit* DRUGGER)
ANANIAS (*talking with* SUBTLE)   Sir, I know
The Spaniard hates the brethren and hath spies
Upon their actions, and that this was one
I make no scruple. But the holy Synod   75
Have been in prayer and meditation for it.
And 'tis revealed no less to them than me
That casting of money is most lawful.
SUBTLE   True.
But here I cannot do it. If the house
Should chance to be suspected, all would out,   80
And we be locked up in the Tower for ever
To make gold there for the state, never come out.
And then are you defeated.
ANANIAS   I will tell
This to the elders and the weaker brethren,
That the whole company of the Separation   85
May join in humble prayer again.
SUBTLE   And fasting.
ANANIAS Yea, for some fitter place. The peace of mind
Rest with these walls.
SUBTLE   Thanks, courteous Ananias.

Exit ANANIAS

FACE What did he come for?
SUBTLE   About casting dollars
Presently out of hand. And so I told him   90
A Spanish minister came here to spy
Against the faithful—
FACE   I conceive. Come, Subtle,
Thou art so down upon the least disaster!
How wouldst thou ha' done if I had not helped thee out?
SUBTLE I thank thee, Face, for the angry boy, i' faith.   95
FACE Who would ha' looked it should ha' been that rascal
Surly? He had dyed his beard and all. Well, sir,
Here's damask come to make you a suit.
SUBTLE   Where's Drugger?

68. *credit with the players*: with the actors.
70. *help it*: bring it about.
71. *Hieronymo's old cloak*: Hieronymo is the leading character in Kyd's
    melodramatic revenge play, *The Spanish Tragedy*.
92. *I conceive*: I understand.

FACE　He is gone to borrow me a Spanish habit.
I'll be the Count now.
SUBTLE　　　　　　　But where's the widow?　　　　100
FACE　Within with my lord's sister; Madame Dol
Is entertaining her.
SUBTLE　　　　　　By your favour, Face,
Now she is honest, I will stand again.
FACE　You will not offer it?
SUBTLE　　　　　　　Why?
FACE　　　　　　　　　Stand to your word
Or—here comes Dol. She knows—
SUBTLE　　　　　　　　You are tyrannous still.　　105

Enter DOL *hastily*

FACE　Strict for my right. How now, Dol? Hast told her
The Spanish Count will come?
DOL　　　　　　　　Yes, but another is come
You little looked for!
FACE　　　　　　Who's that?
DOL　　　　　　　　Your master:
The master of the house.
SUBTLE　　　　　How, Dol?
FACE　　　　　　　　She lies.
This is some trick. Come, leave your quiblins, Dorothy.　　110
DOL　Look out and see.　(FACE *goes to the window*)
SUBTLE　　　　　Art thou in earnest?
DOL　　　　　　　　　'Slight,
Forty o' the neighbours are about him, talking.
FACE　'Tis he, by this good day.
DOL　　　　　　　'Twill prove ill day
For some on us.
FACE　　　　We are undone and taken!
DOL　Lost, I'm afraid.
SUBTLE　　　　　You said he would not come　　115
While there died one a week within the liberties.
FACE　No, 'twas within the walls.
SUBTLE　　　　　　　Was't so? Cry you mercy.
I thought the liberties. What shall we do now, Face?
FACE　Be silent. Not a word if he call or knock.
I'll into mine old shape again and meet him　　120
Of Jeremy the butler. I' the meantime
Do you two pack up all the goods and purchase
That we can carry i' the two trunks. I'll keep him

103. *honest*: 'now that I know she is not a whore'.
110. *quiblins*: tricks.
116. *liberties*: districts outside the City boundaries but still under the
　　municipal authority.

Off for today if I cannot longer, and then
At night, I'll ship you both away to Ratcliff,   125
Where we'll meet tomorrow and there we'll share.
Let Mammon's brass and pewter keep the cellar;
We'll have another time for that. But, Dol,
Pray thee, go heat a little water quickly.
Subtle must shave me. All my captain's beard   130
Must off to make me appear smooth Jeremy.
You'll do't?

SUBTLE   Yes, I'll shave you as well as I can.

FACE   And not cut my throat, but trim me?

SUBTLE   You shall see, sir.

Exeunt

125. *Ratcliff*: along the river, in Stepney.
130. *shave me*: a play on the slang meaning of 'to cheat' or 'do down'. See
    Dekker's *The Seven Deadly Sins of London* where the extortionate exploita-
    tion of the poor is treated under this heading.

ACT V

Scene 1 : *Before Lovewit's door*

Enter LOVEWIT *with several neighbours*

LOVEWIT   Has there been such resort, say you?
NEIGHBOUR 1   Daily, sir.
NEIGHBOUR 2   And nightly too.
NEIGHBOUR 3   Ay, some as brave as lords.
NEIGHBOUR 4   Ladies and gentlewomen.
NEIGHBOUR 5   Citizen's wives,
NEIGHBOUR 1   And knights.
NEIGHBOUR 6   In coaches.
NEIGHBOUR 2   Yes, and oister women.
NEIGHBOUR 1   Beside other gallants.
NEIGHBOUR 3   Sailors' wives.
NEIGHBOUR 4   Tobacco men. 5
NEIGHBOUR 5   Another Pimlico!
LOVEWIT   What should my knave
                                              [advance
To draw this company? He hung out no banners
Of a strange calf with five legs to be seen?
Or a huge lobster with six claws?
NEIGHBOUR 6   No, sir.
NEIGHBOUR 3   We had gone in then, sir.
LOVEWIT   He has no gift   10
Of teaching i' the nose that ere I knew of!
You saw no bills set up that promised cure
Of agues or the tooth-ache?
NEIGHBOUR 2   No such thing, sir.
LOVEWIT   Nor heard a drum struck for baboons or puppets?
NEIGHBOUR 5   Neither, sir.
LOVEWIT   What device should he bring forth
                                              [now? 15
I love a teeming wit as I love my nourishment.

2. *brave*: finely dressed and with courteous manners.
6. *Pimlico*: a house famous for cakes and ale.
10. *We had gone in*: 'If that had been the case, we would have gone inside.'
12. *bills set up*: as a mountebank would set up advertisements of the cures he claimed to have accomplished.
14. *drum struck* etc.: Drum rolls and the blowing of a trumpet would announce the opening of a show. Baboons were sometimes put on exhibition; 'a great baboon' was shown in Southwark in the early sixteen-hundreds, to the disgust of actors of 'the legitimate stage' and of Jonson himself (see *Discoveries*, 608–11).

Pray God he ha' not kept such open house
That he hath sold my hangings and my bedding.
I left him nothing else. If he have eat 'em,
A plague o' the moth, say I. Sure he has got   20
Some bawdy pictures to call this ging:
The friar and the nun, or the new motion
Of the knight's courser covering the parson's mare,
The boy of six year old with the great thing,
Or 't may be he has the fleas that run at tilt   25
Upon a table, or some dog to dance.
When saw you him?

NEIGHBOUR 1   Who, sir? Jeremy?
NEIGHBOUR 2   Jeremy butler?
We saw him not this month.

LOVEWIT   How?
NEIGHBOUR 4   Not these five weeks, sir.
NEIGHBOUR 1   These six weeks at the least.
LOVEWIT   You amaze me,
                                            [neighbours!
NEIGHBOUR 5   Sure, if your worship know not where he is,   30
He's slipped away.

NEIGHBOUR 6   Pray God he be not made away!
LOVEWIT   Ha! It's no time to question, then. (*he knocks*)
NEIGHBOUR 6   About
Some three weeks since, I heard a doleful cry
As I sat up a-mending my wife's stockings.

LOVEWIT   This is strange, that none will answer! Didst thou
                                            [hear 35
A cry, sayest thou?

NEIGHBOUR 6   Yes, sir, like unto a man
That had been strangled an hour and could not speak.

NEIGHBOUR 2   I heard it too, just this day three weeks at two
                                            [o'clock
Next morning.

LOVEWIT   These be miracles, or you make 'em so!
A man an hour strangled and could not speak,   40
And both you heard him cry?

NEIGHBOUR 3   Yes, downward, sir.

---

21. *ging*: crowd.
22. *The friar and the nun*: probably as in Thomas Heywood's play *If You Know not Me* (1606): 'here's the Friar whipping the nun's arse'.
  the new motion: new puppet-play.
24. *the boy*: cf. one of the Wife's reminiscences in *The Knight of the Burning Pestle*: 'Of all the sights that ever were in London since I was married, me thinks the little child that was so fair grown about the members was the prettiest; that, and the hermaphrodite.'
31. *not made away*: not murdered.

LOVEWIT   Thou art a wise fellow. Give me thy hand, I pray
                                                    [thee.
What trade art thou on?
NEIGHBOUR 3   A smith, an't please your worship.
LOVEWIT   A smith? Then lend me thy help to get this door open.
NEIGHBOUR 3   That I will presently, sir, but fetch my tools—
                                                [(*exit*) 45
NEIGHBOUR 1   Sir, best to knock again afore you break it.
LOVEWIT   I will.

Scene 2

Enter FACE *in his butler's livery*

FACE   What mean you, sir?
NEIGHBOURS 1, 2, 4   Oh, here's Jeremy!
FACE   Good sir, come from the door.
LOVEWIT   Why, what's the matter?
FACE   Yet farther. You are too near yet.
LOVEWIT   I' the name of wonder!
What means the fellow?
FACE   The house, sir, has been visited.
LOVEWIT   What? With the plague? Stand thou then farther.
FACE   No, sir,   5
I had it not.
LOVEWIT   Who had it then? I left
None else but thee i' the house!
FACE   Yes, sir. My fellow,
The cat that kept the buttery had it on her
A week before I spied it, but I got her
Conveyed away i' the night. And so I shut   10
The house up for a month—
LOVEWIT   How?
FACE   Purposing then, sir,
T'have burnt rose-vinegar, treacle and tar,
And ha' made it sweet that you should ne'er ha' known it,
Because I knew the news would but afflict you, sir.
LOVEWIT   Breathe less, and farther off. Why, this is stranger!   15
The neighbours tell me all, here, that the doors
Have still been open—
FACE   How, sir?
LOVEWIT   Gallants, men and women,
And of all sorts, tag-rag, been seen to flock here
In threaves these ten weeks, as to a second Hogsden

---

19. *threaves*: droves.
    Hogsden: Hoxton, a favourite City holiday resort (Jonson killed the actor
    Gabriel Spencer in Hoxton Fields. See Introduction p. 20).

In days of Pimlico and Eye-bright!

FACE   Sir,   20
Their wisdoms will not say so!

LOVEWIT   Today, they speak
Of coaches and gallants; one in a French hood
Went in, they tell me. And another was seen
In a velvet gown at the window! Divers more
Pass in and out!

FACE   They did pass through the doors, then,   25
Or walls, I assure their eyesights, and their spectacles.
For here, sir, are the keys. And here have been
In this my pocket now above twenty days!
And for before, I kept the fort alone there.
But that 'tis yet not deep i' the afternoon,   30
I should believe my neighbours had seen double
Through the black-pot, and made these apparitions!
For, on my faith to your worship, for these three weeks
And upwards, the door has not been opened.

LOVEWIT   Strange!

NEIGHBOUR 1   Good faith, I think I saw a coach!

NEIGHBOUR 2   And I, too,   35
I'd ha' been sworn!

LOVEWIT   Do you but think it now?
And but one coach?

NEIGHBOUR 4   We cannot tell, sir. Jeremy
Is a very honest fellow.

FACE   Did you see me at all?

NEIGHBOUR 1   No. That we are sure on.

NEIGHBOUR 2   I'll be sworn o' that.

LOVEWIT   Fine rogues, to have your testimonies built on!   40

Re-enter NEIGHBOUR 3 *with his tools*

NEIGHBOUR 3   Is Jeremy come?

NEIGHBOUR 1   Oh yes, you may leave your tools.
We were deceived, he says.

NEIGHBOUR 2   He has had the keys,
And the door has been shut these three weeks.

NEIGHBOUR 3   Like enough.

LOVEWIT   Peace, and get hence, you changelings.

Enter SURLY *and* MAMMON

FACE (*aside*)   Surly come!
And Mammon made acquainted! They'll tell all.   45
How shall I beat them off? What shall I do?
Nothing's more wretched than a guilty conscience.

20. *Eye-bright*: like Pimlico, famous for its beer.
44. *changelings*: idiots, dim-wits.

Scene 3

SURLY (*to* MAMMON)   No, sir, he was a great physician! This,
It was no bawdy house, but a mere chancel!
You knew the lord and his sister!
MAMMON   Nay, good Surly—
SURLY   The happy word, 'Be rich'—
MAMMON   Play not the tyrant—
SURLY   Should be today pronounced to all your friends!   5
And where be your andirons now? And your brass pots?
That should ha' been golden flagons and great wedges.
MAMMON   Let me but breathe. What! They ha' shut their doors,
Methinks! (MAMMON *and* SURLY *knock*)
SURLY   Ay, now 'tis holiday with them.
MAMMON   Rogues!
Cozeners, impostors, bawds!
FACE (*goes up to them*)   What mean you, sir?   10
MAMMON   To enter if we can.
FACE   Another man's house?
Here is the owner, sir. Turn you to him
And speak your business.
MAMMON   Are you, sir, the owner?
LOVEWIT   Yes, sir.
MAMMON   And are those knaves within your cheaters?
LOVEWIT   What knaves? What cheaters?
MAMMON   Subtle, and his Lungs. 15
FACE   The gentleman is distracted, sir! No lungs
Nor lights ha' been seen here these three weeks, sir,
Within these doors, upon my word.
SURLY   Your word,
Groom arrogant?
FACE   Yes, sir. I am the house-keeper
And know the keys ha' not been out o' my hands.   20
SURLY   This is a new Face!
FACE   You do mistake the house, sir!
What sign was't at?
SURLY   You rascal! This is one
O' the confederacy. Come, let's get officers
And force the door.
LOVEWIT   Pray you stay, gentlemen.

2. *mere chancel*: as pure as a church (the chancel leads to the sanctuary).
7. *great wedges*: ingots of gold and silver.
16–17. *lungs nor lights*: pun taking up 'lights' as cat-food (Face having got
    rid of the cat who, according to him, was infected with the plague).
22. *What sign*: painted signs hung from tradesmen's shops, and ale and
    eating houses. Face pretends to be testing Surly on his identification of the
    house.

SURLY   No, sir, we'll come with warrant.
MAMMON   Ay, and then   25
We shall ha' your doors open.

Exeunt MAMMON *and* SURLY

LOVEWIT   What means this?
FACE   I cannot tell, sir!
NEIGHBOUR I   These are two o' the gallants
That we do think we saw.
FACE   Two o' the fools?
You talk as idly as they. Good faith, sir,
I think the moon has crazed 'em all!   30

Enter KASTRIL

FACE (*aside*)   Oh me,
The angry boy come too? He'll make a noise
And ne'er away till he have betrayed us all.
KASTRIL (*knocking*)   What, rogues, bawds, slaves! You'll open
                                        [the door anon.
Punk, cocatrice, my suster! By this light,
I'll fetch the Marshal to you. You are a whore   35
To keep your castle—
FACE   Who would you speak with, sir?
KASTRIL   The bawdy Doctor and the cozening Captain,
And puss my suster.
LOVEWIT   This is something, sure!
FACE (*to* LOVEWIT)   Upon my trust, the doors were never open,
                                        [sir.
KASTRIL   I have heard all their tricks, told me twice over   40
By the fat knight and the lean gentleman.
LOVEWIT   Here comes another.

Enter ANANIAS *and* TRIBULATION

FACE (*aside*)   Ananias too,
And his Pastor!
TRIBULATION   The doors are shut against us.
ANANIAS.   Come forth, you seed of sulphur, sons of fire!
                              (*they both beat at the door*)
Your stench, it is broke forth. Abomination   45
Is in the house.
KASTRIL   Ay, my suster's there!
ANANIAS   The place
It is become a cage of unclean birds.
KASTRIL   Yes, I will fetch the scavenger and the constable.

---

34. *cocatrice*: the basilisk, supposed to kill by a glance and to be hatched
from a cock's egg. Term often applied to a whore or a loose woman.

TRIBULATION You shall do well.
ANANIAS   We'll join, to weed them out.
KASTRIL (*shouting*) You will not come then? Punk device, my
[suster! 50
ANANIAS Call her not sister. She is a harlot, verily.
KASTRIL I'll raise the street.
LOVEWIT   Good gentlemen, a word.
ANANIAS Satan, avoid, and hinder not our zeal.

Exeunt ANANIAS, TRIBULATION *and* KASTRIL

LOVEWIT The world's turned Bedlam.
FACE   These are all broke loose
Out of Saint Katherine's, where they use to keep   55
The better sort of mad-folks.
NEIGHBOUR 1   All these persons
We saw go in and out here.
NEIGHBOUR 2   Yes indeed, sir.
NEIGHBOUR 3 These were the parties.
FACE   Peace, you drunkards.
[Sir,
I wonder at it! Please you to give me leave
To touch the door. I'll try an the lock be changed.   60
LOVEWIT It 'mazes me!
FACE   Good faith, sir, I believe
There's no such thing. 'Tis all *deceptio visus*.
(*aside*) Would I could get him away!

(DAPPER *cries out from inside*)

DAPPER   Master Captain, master
[Doctor!
LOVEWIT Who's that?
FACE (*aside*) Our clerk within, that I forgot! (*to* LOVEWIT)
[I know not, sir.
DAPPER For God's sake, when will her Grace be at leisure?
FACE   Ha! 65
Illusions, some spirit o' the air. (*aside*) His gag is melted,
And now he sets out the throat.
DAPPER   I am almost stifled!
FACE (*aside*) Would you were altogether.
LOVEWIT   'Tis i' the house.
Ha! List!
FACE Believe it, sir, i' the air!

---

50. *punk device*: 'device' was commonly used as an intensive (meaning here
'absolute whore' or 'arrant whore').
55. *Saint Katherine's*: an old hospital for the physically and mentally sick,
founded in the twelfth century.
62. *deceptio visus*: optical illusion.

LOVEWIT   Peace, you—
DAPPER   My aunt's Grace does not use me well
SUBTLE (*in the house*)   You fool,   70
Peace, you'll mar all.
FACE   Or you will else, you rogue.
LOVEWIT   Oh, is it so? Then you converse with spirits!
Come, sir. No more o' your tricks, good Jeremy.
The truth, the shortest way.
FACE   Dismiss this rabble, sir.
(*aside*) What shall I do? I am catched.
LOVEWIT   Good neighbours,   75
I thank you all. You may depart.

Exeunt neighbours

(*to* FACE)   Come, sir,
You know that I am an indulgent master,
And therefore, conceal nothing. What's your medicine
To draw so many several sorts of wild-fowl?
FACE   Sir, you were wont to affect mirth and wit—
But here's no place to talk on't i' the street.   80
Give me but leave to make the best of my fortune
And only pardon me th' abuse of your house.
It's all I beg. I'll help you to a widow
In recompense, that you shall gi' me thanks for,
Will make you seven years younger, and a rich one.   85
'Tis but your putting on a Spanish cloak.
I have her within. You need not fear the house:
It was not visited.
LOVEWIT   But by me, who came
Sooner than you expected.
FACE   It is true, sir.
Pray you forgive me.
LOVEWIT   Well, let's see your widow.   90

They go inside the house

Scene 4: *A room in Lovewit's house*

Enter SUBTLE, *leading in* DAPPER *with his eyes bound as before*

SUBTLE   How! Ha' you eaten your gag?
DAPPER   Yes, faith, it crumbled
Away in my mouth.
SUBTLE   You ha' spoilt all, then.

74. *the truth*: 'Come and tell me the truth: you'll find it's the shortest way
   out of your difficulties.'
79. *wont to affect mirth and wit*: 'You were always a person noted for having
   a sense of humour, a liking for fun and inventiveness.'
88. *not visited*: i.e. by the plague.

DAPPER   No,
I hope my aunt of Fairy will forgive me.
SUBTLE   Your aunt's a gracious lady, but in troth
You were to blame.
DAPPER   The fume did overcome me,   5
And I did do't to stay my stomach. Pray you,
So satisfy her Grace.

Enter FACE *in his uniform*

          Here comes the Captain.
FACE   How now? Is his mouth down?
SUBTLE   Ay, he has spoken.
FACE (*aside to* SUBTLE)   A pox! I heard him, and you too.
(*aloud*) He's undone then.
(*aside*) I have been fain to say the house is haunted.   10
With spirits, to keep the churl back.
SUBTLE   And hast thou done it?
FACE   Sure, for this night.
SUBTLE   Why then, triumph and sing
Of Face so famous, the precious king
Of present wits.
FACE   Did you not hear the coil
About the door?
SUBTLE   Yes, and I dwindled with it.   15
FACE   Show him his aunt, and let him be dispatched.
I'll send her to you. (*exit*)
SUBTLE   Well, sir, your aunt, her Grace,
Will give you audience presently on my suit
And the Captain's word that you did not eat your gag
In any contempt of her Highness. (*unbinds his eyes*)
DAPPER   Not I, in troth, sir.   20

Enter DOL *like the Queen of Fairy*

SUBTLE   Here she is come. Down o' your knees and wriggle.
She has a stately presence. Good. Yet nearer,
And bid 'God save you'.
DAPPER   Madam.
SUBTLE   And your aunt.
DAPPER   And my most gracious aunt, God save your Grace.
DOL   Nephew, we thought to have been angry with you,   25
But that sweet face of yours hath turned the tide
And made it flow with joy that ebbed of love.
Arise, and touch our velvet gown.
SUBTLE   The skirts,
And kiss 'em. So.
DOL   Let me now stroke that head.

14. *coil*: noise, confusion.

Much, nephew, shalt thou win, much shalt thou spend;   30
Much shalt thou give away, much shalt thou lend.
SUBTLE (*aside*)   Ay, much indeed. (*aloud*) Why do you not
                                        [thank her Grace?
DAPPER   I cannot speak for joy.
SUBTLE   See the kind wretch!
Your Grace's kinsman right.
DOL   Give me the bird.
Here is your fly in a purse about your neck, cousin.   35
Wear it and feed it about this day sev'night,
On your right wrist—
SUBTLE   Open a vein with a pin
And let it suck but once a week. Till then
You must not look on't.
DOL   No. And, kinsman,
Bear yourself worthy of the blood you come on.   40
SUBTLE   Her Grace would ha' you eat no more Woolsack pies,
Nor Dagger frumity.
DOL   Nor break his fast
In Heaven and Hell.
SUBTLE   She's with you everywhere!
Nor play with costermongers at mum-chance, tray-trip,
God-make-you-rich (when as your aunt has done it), but keep   45
The gallant'st company, and the best games—
DAPPER   Yes, sir.
SUBTLE   Gleek and primero. And what you get, be true to us.
DAPPER   By this hand, I will.
SUBTLE   You may bring's a thousand pound
Before tomorrow night, if but three thousand
Be stirring, an you will.
DAPPER   I swear I will, then.   50
SUBTLE   Your fly will learn you all games.
FACE (*off-stage*)   Ha' you done there?

41. *Woolsack pies*: The Woolsack was an inn and eating-house in Ivy Lane,
    famous, like The Dagger, for its pies.
42. *frumity*: one of the forms of 'frumenty' or 'furmety', a dish made of
    wheat boiled in milk and seasoned with spices and vinegar. (Cf. Hardy's
    Mayor of Casterbridge where Henchard sells his wife in the furmety
    woman's booth.) 'Dagger frumity' means furmety as made at the Dagger,
    probably well laced with spirits.
43. *Heaven and Hell*: the names of two taverns on the site of the present
    committee rooms of the House of Commons.
44. *mum-chance*: both a card and a dice game, played in silence: hence its
    name. Popular with costermongers.
    tray-trip: another dice game, in which three (tray) was the best throw.
45. *God-make-you-rich*: backgammon.
47. *Gleek and primero*: gleek was a card game for three players, in which one
    tried for a set of three court-cards of the same kind (gleek = German
    'gleich', alike). Primero: another card game, four being dealt to each
    player.

SUBTLE   Your Grace will command him no more duties?
DOL   No.
But come and see me often. I may chance
To leave him three or four hundred chests of treasure
And some twelve thousand acres of fairyland,   55
If he game well and comely, with good gamesters!
SUBTLE   There's a kind aunt! Kiss her departing part.
But you must sell your forty mark a year, now.
DAPPER   Ay, sir, I mean.
SUBTLE   Or gi't away. Pox on't!
DAPPER   I'll gi't mine aunt. I'll go and fetch the writings.   60

Exit DAPPER

SUBTLE   'Tis well, away!

Re-enter FACE

FACE   Where's Subtle?
SUBTLE   Here. What news?
FACE   Drugger is at the door. Go take his suit
And bid him fetch a parson presently.
Say he shall marry the widow. Thou shalt spend
A hundred pound by the service! (*exit* SUBTLE) Now, queen
                                                        [Dol,   65
Ha' you packed up all?
DOL   Yes.
FACE   And how do you like
The lady Pliant?
DOL   A good dull innocent.

Re-enter SUBTLE

SUBTLE   Here's your Hieronymo's cloak and hat.
FACE   Give me 'em.
SUBTLE   And the ruff too?
FACE   Yes, I'll come to you presently.

Exit FACE

SUBTLE   Now he is gone about his project, Dol,   70
I told you of, for the widow.
DOL   'Tis direct
Against our articles.
SUBTLE   Well, we'll fit him, wench.
Hast thou gulled her of her jewels or her bracelets?
DOL   No, but I will do't.
SUBTLE   Soon, at night, my Dolly,

72. *against our articles*: against the terms of the agreement made between the
three and renewed, for instance, in the opening scene (Cf. p. 36, ll. 132–6),
the 'venture tripartite'.
fit him: be a match for him.
K

When we are shipped and all our goods aboard   75
Eastward for Ratcliff, we will turn our course
To Brainford, westward, if thou sayest the word,
And take our leaves of this o'erweaning rascal,
This peremptory Face.
DOL   Content, I am weary of him.
SUBTLE   Thou hast cause, when the slave will run a-wiving,
                                                    [Dol,   80
Against the instrument that was drawn between us.
DOL   I'll pluck this bird as bare as I can.
SUBTLE   Yes, tell her
She must by any means address some present
To the cunning man. Make him amends for wronging
His art with her suspicion. Send a ring   85
Or chain of pearl. She will be tortured else
Extremely in her sleep, say, and ha' strange things
Come to her. Wilt thou?
DOL   Yes.
SUBTLE   My fine flitter-mouse,
My bird o' the night! We'll tickle it at the Pigeons
When we have all and may unlock the trunks   90
And say this is mine, and thine, and thine, and mine.
                                        [(*they kiss*)

Re-enter FACE

FACE   What now, a-billing?
SUBTLE   Yes, a little exalted
In the good passage of our stock-affairs.
FACE   Drugger has brought his parson. Take him in, Subtle,
And send Nab back again to wash his face.   95
SUBTLE   I will. And shave himself?
FACE   If you can get him.

Exit SUBTLE

DOL   You are hot upon it, Face, whate'er it is!
FACE   A trick that Dol shall spend ten pound a month by.

Re-enter SUBTLE

Is he gone?
SUBTLE   The chaplain waits you i' the hall, sir.

77. *Brainford*: Brentford in Middlesex.
81. *instrument . . . drawn between us*: again the agreement that was drawn up.
88. *flitter-mouse*: bat (German 'Fledermaus').
89. *the Pigeons*: inn at Brentford which stood till 1916. The scene of Tony
   Lumpkin's drinking party in *She Stoops to Conquer*.
93. *stock-affairs*: the progress of our joint interests. Subtle is rubbing it in
   that everything they have gained is to be shared among the three.

FACE   I'll go bestow him. *(exit)*

DOL   He'll now marry her, instantly.   100

SUBTLE   He cannot yet, he is not ready. Dear Dol,
Cozen her of all thou canst. To deceive him
Is no deceit but justice, that would break
Such an inextricable tie as ours was.

DOL   Let me alone to fit him.

Re-enter FACE

FACE   Come, my venturers,   105
You ha' packed up all? Where be the trunks?

                                        Bring forth.

SUBTLE   Here.

FACE   Let's see 'em. Where's the money?

SUBTLE   Here,
In this.

FACE   Mammon's ten pound. Eight score before.
The brethren's money, this. Drugger's and Dapper's.
What paper's that?

DOL   The jewel of the waiting maid's   110
That stole it from her lady to know certain—

FACE   If she should have precedence of her mistress?

DOL   Yes.

FACE   What box is that?

SUBTLE   The fish-wife's rings, I think.
And the ale-wife's single money. Is't not, Dol?

DOL   Yes. And the whistle that the sailor's wife   115
Brought you, to know an her husband were with Ward.

FACE   We'll wet it tomorrow, and our silver beakers
And tavern cups. Where be the French petticoats
And girdles and hangers?

SUBTLE   Here, i' the trunk.
And the bolts of lawn.

FACE   Is Drugger's damask there?   120
And the tobacco?

SUBTLE   Yes.

FACE   Give me the keys.

DOL   Why you the keys?

SUBTLE   No matter, Dol: because
We shall not open 'em before he comes.

FACE   'Tis true you shall not open them indeed,
Nor have 'em forth. Do you see? Not forth, Dol.   125

114. *single money*: coins of little value.
116. *Ward*: a famous pirate whose exploits were in the public eye at this
    time. Wives would be anxious if they thought their sailor husbands
    might be in such dangerous company.
120. *bolts of lawn*: rolls of a fine woven fabric.

DOL   No.
FACE   No, my smock-rampant. The right is, my master
Knows all, has pardoned me, and he will keep 'em.
Doctor, 'tis true, you look, for all your figures.
I sent for him, indeed. Wherefore, good partners,
Both he and she, be satisfied. For here   130
Determines the indenture tripartite
'Twixt Subtle, Dol and Face. All I can do
Is to help you over the wall o'the backside,
Or lend you a sheet to save your velvet gown, Dol.
Here will be officers presently. Bethink you   135
Of some course suddenly to 'scape the dock,
For thither you'll come else. (*knocking heard*)
                                        Hark you, thunder!
SUBTLE   You are a precious fiend!
OFFICER (*outside*)   Open the door!
FACE   Dol, I am sorry for thee, i'faith. But, hear'st thou,
It shall go hard, but I will place thee somewhere.   140
Thou shalt ha' my letter to Mistress Amo.
DOL   Hang you—
FACE   Or Madam Caesarean.
DOL   Pox upon you, rogue!
Would I had but time to beat thee.
FACE   Subtle,
Let's know where you set up next. I'll send you
A customer now and then for old acquaintance.   145
What new course ha' you?
SUBTLE   Rogue, I'll hang myself,
That I may walk a greater devil than thou,
And haunt thee i' the flock-bed and the buttery.

Exeunt

126. *smock-rampant*: Dol is looking like a heraldic device, frozen into
immobility for a moment because of Face's unexpected *coup*. 'Smock' (an
undergarment) is here a knowing-playful term like 'baggage': 'rampant'
because she has just been so active, and is about to be so furious.
131. *determines*: terminates.
141–142. *Mistress Amo ... Madam Caesarean*: nicknames for brothel-
keepers. Face means he will give Dol letters of introduction.
148. *flock-bed*: flock was a cheap material used for stuffing mattresses etc.
Both this and 'buttery' must be references to Face's continuing life as a
butler.

Scene 5: An outer room

Enter LOVEWIT *in Spanish dress, with the parson*

Loud knocking at the door

LOVEWIT   What do you mean, my masters?
MAMMON (*outside*)   Open your door,
  Cheaters, bawds, conjurers!
OFFICER (*outside*)   Or we'll break it open.
LOVEWIT   What warrant have you?
OFFICER   Warrant enough, sir, doubt
                                        [not,
  If you'll not open it.
LOVEWIT   Is there an officer there?
OFFICER   Yes, two or three for failing.
LOVEWIT   Have but patience,   5
  And I will open it straight.

Enter FACE *as butler*

FACE   Sir, ha' you done?
  Is it a marriage? Perfect?
LOVEWIT   Yes, my brain.
FACE   Off with your ruff and cloak, then. Be yourself, sir.
SURLY (*outside*)   Down with the door!
KASTRIL (*outside*)   'Slight! Ding it open!
LOVEWIT (*opening the door*)   Hold! Hold, gentlemen. What
                                        [means this violence?   10

MAMMON, SURLY, KASTRIL, ANANIAS, TRIBULATION *and*
                                        [*officers rush in*

MAMMON   Where is this collier?
SURLY   And my Captain Face?
MAMMON   These day-owls.
SURLY   That are birding in men's purses.
MAMMON   Madame Suppository.
KASTRIL   Doxy, my suster.
ANANIAS   Locusts
  Of the foul pit.
TRIBULATION   Profane as Bel and the Dragon.

5. *for failing*: in case a smaller number might fail.
9. *ding*: break. One of Kastril's country terms.
11. *collier*: cheat (see p. 34, l. 90, note).
13. *Suppository*: 'A plug of cylindrical shape to be introduced into the rectum
  in order to stimulate the bowel to action . . . or into the vagina or urethra
  for various purposes' (*O.E.D.*) which also quotes a writer called Markham
  (1610—the year of Jonson's play): 'Nothing can purge the guts with that
  gentleness which a suppository doth.' Also slang for a prostitute.
  doxy: tramp's mistress.
14. *Bel and the Dragon*: an apocryphal book of the Old Testament, considered
  a 'fable' by St. Jerome.

ANANIAS   Worse than the grasshoppers or the lice of Egypt.   15

LOVEWIT   Good gentlemen, hear me. Are you officers,
And cannot stay this violence?

OFFICER   Keep the peace!

LOVEWIT   Gentlemen, what is the matter? Whom do you seek?

MAMMON   The chemical cozener!

SURLY   And the captain pandar!

KASTRIL   The nun, my suster!

MAMMON   Madam Rabbi!

ANANIAS   Scorpions   20
And caterpillars!

LOVEWIT   Fewer at once, I pray you.

OFFICER   One after another, gentlemen, I charge you
By virtue of my staff—

ANANIAS   They are the vessels
Of pride, lust and the cart.

LOVEWIT   Good zeal, lie still
A little while.

TRIBULATION   Peace, Deacon Ananias.   25

LOVEWIT   The house is mine here and the doors are open.
If there be any such persons as you seek for,
Use your authority, search on, o' God's name.
I am but newly come to town, and finding
This tumult 'bout my door, to tell you true,   30
It somewhat 'mazed me, till my man here, fearing
My more displeasure, told me he had done
Somewhat an insolent part, let out my house,
Belike presuming on my own aversion
From any air o' the town while there was sickness,   35
To a doctor and a captain, who what they are
Or where they be he knows not.

MAMMON   Are they gone?

LOVEWIT   You may go in and search, sir. (MAMMON, ANANIAS
and TRIBULATION *go in*) Here I find
The empty walls worse than I left 'em, smoked,
A few cracked pots, and glasses, and a furnace,   40
The ceiling filled with posies of the candle,
And madam with a dildo writ o' the walls.
Only, one gentlewoman I met here
That is within, that said she was a widow—

KASTRIL   Ay, that's my suster. I'll go thump her. Where is
                               [she? (*exit*)   45

20. *Nun*: slang for prostitute.
24. *the cart*: as in p. 124, l. 29, a reference to the penalties of their fraud.
41. *posies of the candle*: in *Philaster* by Beaumont and Fletcher, the King
    tells Megra that 'all the court shall . . . fling rotten oranges, make ribald
    rhymes and sear thy name with candles upon walls'. The 'posy' is a
    phrase or a line of verse, here probably an obscenity of some sort.

LOVEWIT   And should ha' married a Spanish count, but he,
  When he came to't, neglected her so grossly
  That I, a widower, am gone through with her.
SURLY   How? Have I lost her, then?
LOVEWIT   Were you the Don, sir?
  Good faith, now, she does blame you extremely, and says   50
  You swore and told her you had ta'en the pains
  To dye your beard and umber o'er your face,
  Borrowed a suit and ruff, all for her love;
  And then did nothing. What an oversight
  And want of putting-forward, sir, was this!   55
  Well fare an old harquebuzier yet
  Could prime his powder and give fire and hit
  All in a twinkling.
MAMMON (re-entering from the inner rooms)   The whole nest are
                                                        fled!
LOVEWIT   What sort of birds were they?
MAMMON   A kind of choughs,
  Or thievish daws, sir, that have picked my purse   60
  Of eight-score and ten pounds within these five weeks,
  Beside my first materials and my goods
  That lie i' the cellar, which I am glad they ha' left.
  I may have home yet.
LOVEWIT   Think you so, sir?
MAMMON   Ay.
LOVEWIT   By order of law, sir, but not otherwise.   65
MAMMON   Not mine own stuff?
LOVEWIT   Sir, I can take no knowledge
  That they are yours, but by public means.
  If you can bring certificate that you were gulled of 'em,
  Or any formal writ, out of a court,
  That you did cozen yourself, I will not hold them.   70
MAMMON   I'll rather lose 'em.
LOVEWIT   That you shall not, sir,
  By me, in troth. Upon these terms they are yours.
  What? Should they ha' been, sir, turned into gold all?
MAMMON   No. I cannot tell. It may be they should. What
                                                        [then?
LOVEWIT   What a great loss in hope have you sustained!   75
MAMMON   Not I, but the commonwealth has.
FACE   Ay, he would ha'
                                                        [built
  The city new, and made a ditch about it

56. *harquebuzier*: a soldier with an harquebus; a musketeer. Meaning 'Any
  old soldier would teach you that you have to be quicker at taking action
  than this.'
59. *choughs*: a kind of crow.

Of silver should have run with cream from Hogsden,
That every Sunday in Moorfields the younkers,
And tits, and tom-boys should have fed on gratis.   80
MAMMON   I will go mount a turnip-cart and preach
The end o' the world within these two months. Surly,
What, in a dream?
SURLY   Must I needs cheat myself
With that same foolish vice of honesty?
Come, let us go and hearken out the rogues.   85
That Face I'll mark for mine if e're I meet him.
FACE   If I can hear of him, sir, I'll bring you word
Unto your lodging, for in troth they were strangers
To me. I thought 'em honest as myself, sir.

Exeunt MAMMON *and* SURLY

TRIBULATION (*coming back from the inner rooms with* ANANIAS)
'Tis well. The Saints shall not lose all yet. Go,   90
And get some carts—
LOVEWIT   For what, my zealous friends?
ANANIAS   To bear away the portion of the righteous,
Out of this den of thieves.
LOVEWIT   What is that portion?
ANANIAS   The goods, sometimes the orphans', that the brethren
Bought with their silver pence.
LOVEWIT   What, those i' the cellar, 95
The knight Sir Mammon claims?
ANANIAS   I do defy
The wicked Mammon, so do all the brethren,
Thou profane man! I ask thee with what conscience
Thou canst advance that idol against us
That have the seal? Were not the shillings numbered   100
That made the pounds? Were not the pounds told out
Upon the second day of the fourth week
In the eighth month upon the table dormant
The year of the last patience of the Saints,
Six hundred and ten?
LOVEWIT   Mine earnest, vehement botcher,   105
And Deacon also, I cannot dispute with you,
But if you get not away the sooner
I shall confute you with a cudgel.

---

78. *Hogsden*: Hoxton, like Islington, an outlying, rural district, at pleasant
   walking distance from the City of London. (Cf. p. 133, l. 19, note).
80. *tits*: young girls.
100. *the seal*: the seal of righteousness.
103. *table dormant*: permanent side-table.
104. *patience of the Saints*: because waiting patiently for the coming of the
   kingdom in which they should reign.
105. *botcher*: see p. 88, l. 113, note.

ANANIAS   Sir!
TRIBULATION   Be patient, Ananias.
ANANIAS   I am strong
And will stand up, well girt, against an host,   110
That threaten Gad in exile.
LOVEWIT   I shall send you
To Amsterdam to your cellar.
ANANIAS   I will pray there
Against thy house. May dogs defile thy walls!
And wasps and hornets breed beneath thy roof:
This seat of falsehood and this cave of cozenage!   115

Exeunt ANANIAS *and* TRIBULATION

DRUGGER *enters and* LOVEWIT *beats him away*

LOVEWIT   Another too?
DRUGGER   Not I, sir. I am no brother.
LOVEWIT   Away, you Harry Nicholas! Do you talk?

Exit DRUGGER

FACE   No, this was Abel Drugger. (*to the Parson*) Good sir, go
And satisfy him. Tell him all is done.
He stayed too long a-washing of his face.   120
The Doctor, he shall hear of him at Westchester,
And of the Captain, tell him at Yarmouth, or
Some good port-town else, lying for a wind. (*exit Parson*)
If you can get off the angry child now, sir—

Enter KASTRIL *dragging in his sister*

KASTRIL   Come on, you ewe, you ha' matched most sweetly,
                                        [ha' you not?   125
Did not I say I would never ha' you tupped
But by a dubbed boy to make you a lady-tom?
'Slight, you are a mammet! Oh, I could touse you now.
Death, mun you marry with a pox?
LOVEWIT   You lie, boy.
As sound as you, and I am afore-hand with you.
KASTRIL   Anon!   130

111. *Gad in exile*: 'Gad, a troop shall overcome him; but he shall overcome
   at the last' (Genesis, xlix, 9).
117. *Harry Nicholas*: Henrick Niclaes was leader of the anabaptist sect of
   'The Family of Love', which Queen Elizabeth outlawed in 1580.
121. *Westchester*: the City of Chester.
126. *tupped*: having the ewe coupled with the ram.
128. *mammet*: a variant of maumet from Mohammed, hence a false god or
   idol, the term then coming to mean a doll, a puppet, as applied abusively to
   a girl.
   touse: beat, drag about.

LOVEWIT   Come, will you quarrel? I will feize you, sirrah.
Why do you not buckle to your tools?
KASTRIL   God's light,
This is a fine old boy as e'er I saw!
LOVEWIT   What, do you change your copy now? Proceed.
Here stands my dove. Stoop at her if you dare.   135
KASTRIL   'Slight, I must love him. I cannot choose, i'faith,
And I should be hanged for't. Suster, I protest
I honour thee for this match.
LOVEWIT   Oh, do you so, sir?
KASTRIL   Yes, and thou canst take tobacco and drink, old boy,
I'll give her five hundred pound more to her marriage   140
Than her own state.
LOVEWIT   Fill a pipe-full, Jeremy.
FACE   Yes, but go in and take it, sir.
LOVEWIT   We will.
I will be ruled by thee in anything, Jeremy.
KASTRIL   'Slight, thou art not hide-bound! Thou art a Jovy
                                              [boy!
Come, let's in, I pray thee, and take our whiffs.   145
LOVEWIT   Whiff in with your sister, brother boy.

Exeunt KASTRIL *and* DAME PLIANT

                                      That master
That had received such happiness by a servant
In such a widow and with so much wealth,
Were very ungrateful if he would not be
A little indulgent to that servant's wit   150
And help his fortune though with some small strain
Of his own candour. (*advancing to the front of the stage*)
                              [Therefore, gentlemen
And kind spectators, if I have out-stripped
An old man's gravity, or strict canon, think
What a young wife and a good brain may do: 155
Stretch age's truth sometimes, and crack it too.
(*to* FACE) Speak for thyself, knave.
FACE   So I will, sir. (*advancing*)
                                      [Gentlemen,
My part a little fell in this last scene;
Yet 'twas decorum. And though I am clean
Got off from Subtle, Surly, Mammon, Dol,   160

131. *feize*: frighten off.
134. *change your copy*: 'change your tune'.
135. *stoop*: the hawk 'stoops' or descends on its prey.
152. *candour*: honour (literally 'whiteness').
154. *strict canon*: strict laws of good behaviour.
159. *decorum*: appropriate to the character.

Hot Ananias, Dapper, Drugger, all
With whom I traded, yet I put myself
On you, that are my country; and this pelf
Which I have got, if you do quit me, rests
To feast you often, and invite new guests.   165

Exeunt

163. *that are my country*: Face is seeing himself as appealing to a legal jury.
'By God and the country' was the form of words with which a prisoner
pleading not guilty should ask to be tried.

SELECT BIBLIOGRAPHY

Editions of Jonson's works

All readers of Jonson, and more especially his editors, owe the greatest possible debt to the complete edition of his works by C. H. Herford and Percy and Evelyn Simpson, published in eleven volumes (1925-52) by the Oxford University Press. This includes an account of Jonson's life, a critical commentary on each of the plays and a survey of their stage performances, as well as detailed notes and a complete tabling of all textual variants.

Use has also been made, in preparing the present edition, of *The Works of Ben Jonson* edited by William Gifford, nine volumes, London, 1816.

Books and Essays on Jonson

Barish, J. A. *Ben Jonson and the Language of Prose Comedy*, Cambridge, Mass., 1960.

Barish, J. A. (ed.) *Ben Jonson: A Collection of Critical Essays* (Twentieth Century Views), New Jersey, 1963.

Bradbrook, F. W. 'Ben Jonson's Poetry' (in *From Donne to Marvell, A Guide to English Literature*, Vol. 3. Penguin, 1956).

Brown, Douglas. Introduction to *The Alchemist* (edition in the New Mermaids Series, London, 1966).

Duncan, E. H. 'Jonson's Alchemist and the Literature of Alchemy' (*P.M.L.A.* LXI. Sept. 1946, 699–710).

Eliot, T. S. 'Ben Jonson' (essay written in 1919, reprinted in *Selected Essays*, London, 1932).

Enright, D. J. 'Crime and Punishment in Ben Jonson' (*Scrutiny*, IX, iii, 231–48, 1940).

Enright, D. J. 'Poetic Satire and Satire in Verse (A Consideration of Jonson and Massinger)' (*Scrutiny*, XVIII, iii, 211–23, 1951).

Esdaile, K. A. 'Ben Jonson and the Devil Tavern' (*Essays and Studies*, XXIX, 1943).

Gilbert, A. H. *The Symbolic Persons in the Masques of Ben Jonson*, N. Carolina, 1948.

Heffner, Roy L. 'Unifying Symbols in the Comedy of Ben Jonson' (included in *Elizabethan Drama: Modern Essays in Criticism* ed. R. J. Kaufman, New York, 1961).

Howarth, R. G. 'The Alchemist and Epicoene', *Times Literary Supplement*, April 26, 1934.

Johnston, G. B. *Ben Jonson: Poet*, New York, 1948.

Knights, L. C. *Drama and Society in the Age of Jonson*, London, 1937. Reprinted as a Peregrine Book paperback, Penguin, 1962.

Knights, L. C. 'Ben Jonson: Dramatist' (*The Age of Shakespeare, A Guide to English Literature*, Vol. 2, Penguin, 1955).

Ornstein, R. 'The Moral Vision of Ben Jonson's Tragedy' (included in *Elizabethan Drama: Modern Essays in Criticism* ed. R. J. Kaufman, New York, 1961).

Partridge, E. B. *The Broken Compass, A Study of the Major Comedies of Ben Jonson*, New York, 1958.

Sackton, A. H. *Rhetoric as a Dramatic Language in Ben Jonson*, New York, 1948.

Simpson, E. M. 'Jonson and Dickens: a Study in the Comic genius of London' (*Essays and Studies*, XXIX, 1943).

Smith, G. *Ben Jonson* (*English Men of Letters* series), London, 1919.

Talbot, E. W. 'New Light on Ben Jonson's Workmanship' (*Studies in Philology*, XL, 154–85, 1943).

Thayer, C. G. *Ben Jonson: Studies in the Plays*, Oklahoma, 1963.

Background on Elizabethan Life and Theatre

Chambers, E. K. *The Elizabethan Stage* (2 vols), Oxford, 1923.

Dover Wilson, J. (ed.) *Life in Shakespeare's England*, Cambridge, 1911, Penguin, 1944.

Judges, A. V. (ed.) *The Elizabethan Underworld*, London, 1930.

Rowse, A. L. *The England of Elizabeth*, London, 1950.

Stow, J. *A Survay of London*, 1598, 1603, ed. C. L. Kingsford, Oxford, 1908.

Wilson, F. P. *The Plague in Shakespeare's London*, Oxford, 1927. Reprinted Oxford paperback 1963.

Books on Alchemy

Holmyard, E. J. *Alchemy*, Penguin, 1957.

Read, J. *Prelude to Chemistry: an outline of alchemy, its literature and relationships*, London, 1936.

Taylor, F. S. *The Alchemists*, London, 1951.